COTSWOLDS WALKS WITH CHILDREN

This book is dedicated to

Julia, Edward and Kathryn

Whose determined refusal to walk inspired this book!

COTSWOLDS WALKS WITH CHILDREN

Dave Meredith

SIGMA Leisure

Published by Sigma Leisure - an imprint of
Sigma Press, Stobart House, Pontyclerc, Penybanc Road, Ammanford, Carmarthenshire SA18 3HP.

British Library Cataloguing in Publication Data
A CIP record for this book is available from the British Library.

ISBN: 978-1-85058-970-9

Typesetting and Design by: Sigma Press, Ammanford.

Cover photograph:

Photographs: ©Dave Meredith except for the Chalford Donkey, which was used by kind permission of Ian Peters (www.ianpetersphotographer.co.uk)

Maps: © Dave Meredith

Drawings: © Carol Meredith

Printed by: TJ International Ltd, Padstow, Cornwall

Preface

Cotswold walks with children is a book for parents whose children may not be as keen to go walking as they are. The Cotswolds offers some idyllic walking country and is Britain's largest officially designated 'Area of Outstanding Natural Beauty'. This book takes you to all the best places plus a few gems that even the locals aren't aware of.

Each route has been carefully chosen to provide plenty of interest for both parents and children alike. Many walks have safe places for children to paddle, and over half are pushchair friendly.

Paths follow well established rights-of-way and directions are clear enough for an older child to join in the fun by leading the walk. Along the way there are leaves to collect, questions to answer, tick lists and text of interest to children.

None of the walks are more than 5 miles long, and most have a short cut for when little feet get weary. Refreshments and toilets are listed where they are available.

Locations of Walks

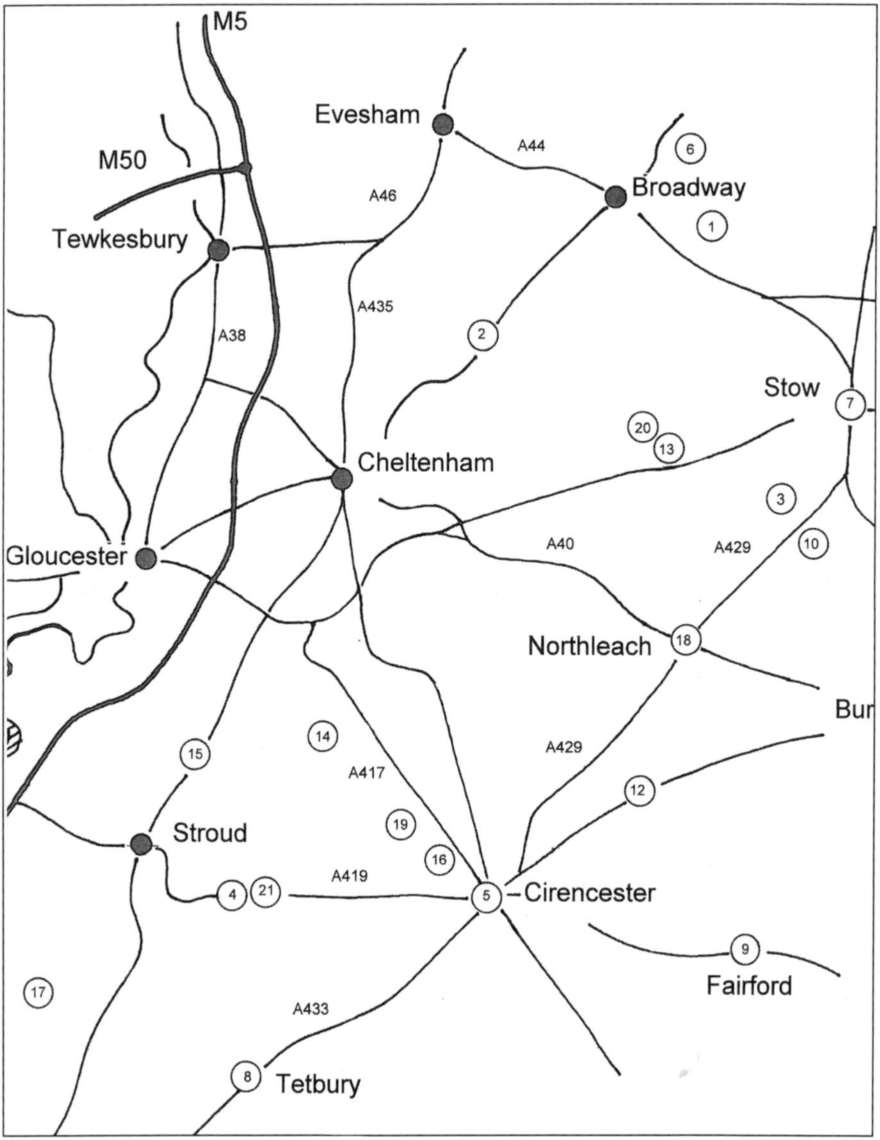

Contents

Thanks to the following test pilots who checked the walks out: June, Rosemary, Shirley, Megan (aged 5) and Robyn (aged 9).

Introduction

Let's make walking fun!

"I'm tired", "How much further is it?" and the usually fatal "I'm bored". These are the cries that strike fear into any parent who wants a few hours in the countryside with their family. It usually means the walk is over - at least as an enjoyable activity.

It needn't be. With a little planning, you will be surprised at just how far you can get them to walk. Eventually, it might be the children who push the parents out of that cosy armchair!

These walks have been written to encourage children to go that extra mile and contain a number of things to maintain their interest.

✓Information in this type is your cue to pass the book to the child so that they can read it for themselves. You could let them lead the walk, taking the precaution of having a photocopy of the walk handy just in case! The secret is to keep them involved, but this will obviously depend on the capability of the child.

- Most walks have a short cut that can be used when little legs get weary.
- Each walk has a checklist that can be completed by a younger child. This can be photocopied to avoid marking the book.
- There are also questions in the text that are aimed at an older child. The answers to these questions are listed at the end of each walk.
- There are also leaves to collect. These are listed with each walk and can be identified using the pictures shown in the book. In winter, you can play nature detective and try to find the dead leaves on the ground.

There are the same number of questions in each category so you can encourage a bit of healthy competition to see who gets the most right!

Both categories are listed in chronological order so it should be possible to plot your progress round the walk, although it may be possible to see some of the check-list items at any stage along the route.

Some games and activities which can be incorporated into a walk:

The Chocolate tree

As an adult you are all powerful and all-knowing. This illusion must be maintained for as long as possible – at least until the children get old enough to realise you are not infallible!

With this game, you tell the children that at the end of the walk there is a magic tree with chocolate growing on it. They, of course, won't believe you, but with a bit of planning you can create a bit of fun and re-assert your omnipotence in the process! After all, this is much more fun than simply giving them their favourite treat, and it means they have an incentive to complete the walk!

At the start, try and identify from which direction the walk finishes and, making sure the children's minds are occupied elsewhere, you can stride off in that direction and plant the chocolate in the branches of a shrub or tree. Make sure it's not too visible from the path otherwise someone else will get the benefit of your little surprise! Return to the start of the walk and keep quiet about the chocolate tree until they start getting tired or bored en-route. As you approach the end of the walk you can start sniffing the air and steering them in the general direction of the hidden treat.

(If you are worried about their diet you could use something else that they like – I once used Christmas crackers on a Boxing Day walk.)

Guess Who

You will need to start the walk armed with a pen and some self adhesive tape. Each child has the name of a TV, cartoon or book character taped to their back. They then ask the child/adult behind them a series of questions in an attempt to identify who the character is. Players can only answer yes or no. The winner is the child who guesses their character in the minimum number of questions.

Seed Mule

Probably more fun with older children and you need another adult with you. Many plants, particularly grasses, propagate their seeds by making them stick to clothing. The children have to see how many of these they can plant on an unsuspecting adult. They will quickly learn that an embrace or cuddle can be used to good effect here!

Another variation is to use acorns or conkers and try and drop them into the hood or pockets of the unwitting adult. They will roar with laughter when a sudden shower causes the hood to be brought into use!

Carrying the apple

Each child tucks an apple or similar object under their chin and attempts to walk as far as they can along the route including stiles and gates. The loser is the first to drop the apple. If more than two children (or even adults) are involved there is a variation where those remaining compete by picking up the dropped apples and adding them to the one they are already carrying under their chin. The winner is the one carrying the most apples! This will at least keep their eyes on the path and stop them from tripping over!

Feeding the ducks

There are few more enchanting experiences for a child than feeding ducks and waterfowl. Traditionally this has been done using bread and similar products such as crackers, chips, donuts - even popcorn. These are a great source of carbohydrate, but they offer little other nutritional value. In fact, bread is the equivalent to junk food for the birds, and too much of it can lead to excessive weight and malnutrition, as well as environmental problems.

In moderation, bread is not harmful to ducks or birds, but that moderation is hard to judge. You might offer the ducks a small amount of bread but there may be other families and individuals arriving after you've left who will also be feeding the ducks. This leads to a diet based almost solely on unhealthy bread products. There are many healthier alternatives to bread. Great choices include:

- Grapes cut in half
- Cracked corn, barley, oats, birdseed or other grains
- Frozen peas that have been defrosted
- Duck feed pellets available from farm supply stores

Be a gourmet bird feeder!

The Boat Race

A traditional favourite, especially in clear fast flowing streams. Each child drops an ice lolly stick or a straw into the stream, and the winner is the first to reach a set position. Works even better with yellow plastic ducks!

Send a Postcard

Many Cotswold villages still have a shop or post office where local postcards may be found. Armed with a pen and a stamp, get the children to fill out a postcard and mail it to a friend or relative. They will enjoy receiving it almost as much as the children will enjoy sending it. They can complain about how arduous the walk is and how many hours have elapsed since they had an ice lolly! Use your imagination – have fun with it!

Invisible ink and elastic bands

Pick a dandelion and look at the stem – a white liquid or sap will be oozing out. You can use this white sap as an invisible ink! Write a secret message on your postcard or in this book. It will be very difficult to read, but once it has dried, it will be clear to see!

Like rubber, the sap of the dandelion contains latex so it can be used to make a small elastic band. Make a wide ring of sap on your little finger. Once it has dried, gently roll it off – it will form a small, stretchy (but not very strong) elastic band. (Do not do this if you think you might be allergic to rubber or latex.)

Gymkhana

You need a few children for this and maybe an adult or two and dry ground!

The children canter along the path like horses. Their hands are held near the waist as if they are holding the reins, and they have to make appropriately encouraging noises to their mounts. The child at the front falls to the ground pretending to be a fence and the other 'horses' jump over it. Once everyone has jumped over, the child leaps back up to continue their ride. As each child reaches the front they pretend to be a fence and so it continues.

Once you have performed this little routine in front of them they will join in enthusiastically.

Be prepared to lose any remaining shreds of dignity.

A flavour of the Cotswolds

Expensive cars rest contentedly on gravel drives, ponies graze happily in grassy paddocks, while burglar alarms, more self-conscious, tuck themselves under the eaves of thatched roofs. These are the more obvious signs of the affluence of Cotswold life. Revealingly, only 1% of the workforce now earns a living from agriculture. It wasn't always so.

Less than a century ago, the Cotswolds was an impoverished region. Rural life was harsh and uncomfortable, though not unhappy, but a series of agricultural depressions in the 19th century proved too much to bear. Farm workers, queuing up for parish relief and charity handouts, drifted away from their decaying cottages. They headed to the towns for regular employment, while the villages fell into a state of dereliction and disrepair.

The very remoteness of many of these villages served to preserve their unique charm. The arrival of the motor car in the 20th century opened up the Cotswolds to people who had grown tired of city life and had the means to escape. They arrived from urban areas and restored property that had been long neglected or derelict. Barns were converted, and smaller cottages amalgamated into larger ones.

The Cotswolds became a desirable place to live and could suddenly count members of the Royal Family among its residents.

While it may be pleasantly cosy to think that the Cotswold villages we see today have remained unchanged, the reality is very different. The only building to provide any continuity through the ages was the church, which stood at the heart of village life. They were the villages' largest and oldest buildings, and in an age when life could be hard and unforgiving, they could be places of rejoicing, regularly the focus of the community.

Apart from the churches, which served as ancient repositories for items of value or curiosity, most of the Cotswold's historic buildings date back to the boom times of the wool trade. This expanded to the point where the prosperity of the whole region depended on it.

England's virtual monopoly of the wool trade in the Middle Ages was mainly due to two factors. The extermination of the wolf (which still flourished in Europe) and the fact that our island enjoyed relative peace, while the continent became battle ground for one war after another. English wool was prized throughout medieval Europe, and merchants from Italy and Flanders bought it in huge quantities. Although not the most valuable of the English wools, it was the shear quantity of good wool that made the Cotswolds the 'Golden Fleece' of medieval England. The Cotswolds had three advantages: extensive sheep pasture, a supply of soft water for washing, scouring and dyeing, and water power to drive the machinery. It has been suggested that around half a million sheep grazed the Cotswolds in the 13th century, and foreign buyers would visit the area to purchase wool years in advance. Many place names are evocative of those times: Washpool, Dyers Lane, Rack Hill, etc.

Merchants became fabulously wealthy on the back of the wool trade and many built beautiful houses, notably William Grevel's at Chipping Campden. Many of their memorial brasses are displayed in the proud Cotswold churches they largely paid for.

Even in times of prosperity, some villages on the exposed uplands struggled to survive the thin margin between life and death. Their populations dwindled and disappeared through a combination of climate change, poor harvests, increased taxation and finally, in 1348/9, the Black Death. In many villages as much as three-quarters of the population died. Many families left the high Cotswolds for the Severn valley, never to return. This caused a decline in arable farming in favour of wool alone – there were simply not enough people left to cultivate the land. These lost villages are indicated on the map as 'Medieval Village of…' and survive as little more than a few bumps, ridges and hollows in the ground.

The high duties on raw wool meant that, after about 1440, cloth exports exceeded wool exports for the first time, and soon woollen cloth became England's major export product. By the late fifteenth century cloth-making was a well established rural industry over much of the Cotswolds, organised by capitalist clothiers who bought and owned the wool. They arranged for all the work, except fulling, to be done in the workers' own homes, usually with their own tools and looms.

Cloth-making is a complex process involving a number of local craftsmen, each responsible for only a part of the process. It was a dawn-till-dusk operation that would involve the whole family. After shearing the wool was combed to remove short fibres, prior to being spun by hand, on spinning wheels in the workers own cottages.

Ten spinners were needed to provide sufficient yarn to keep one weaver employed. Almost every woman spun, but the unmarried ones generally had more time for it so they were known as 'spinsters'.

The resulting yarn was then passed to the cottages of the weavers. Most weavers were illiterate and identified their work by weaving their mark on the edge of the cloth. The cloth of the best weavers was highly prized and would be passed down through the generations.

After weaving, the cloth was fulled using fullers earth. This was a process where the open mesh created by the weaver was shrunk and thickened into cloth. Workers variously called fullers, tuckers or walkers, carried out this laborious task by treading the cloth hour after hour in an alkaline solution. Teasels, the natural kind found alongside any country track, would then be used to raise the nap or fluff. This raised fluff was then shorn using a machine similar to a lawnmower. It was then dyed and dried on racks in the fields to give it 'tenter' or tension. It was this part of the process that added 'tenterhooks' to our vocabulary.

By the turn of the 16th century the cloth trade moved away from woollens to worsteds, and there was a geographic shift in the trade away from the Cotswolds. Here the industry largely died out except for the southern area around Stroud and Dursley, where it continued to flourish. Here, swift streams powered great mills, palaces of industry where huge looms rattled in dusty halls. Water power was later supplemented by coal, which was brought in by canal and rail. At the peak of the cloth trade there were around 150 mills in the Stroud area. A few mills still stand brooding and empty among the ferns and mosses of their damp dark valleys, but most have proved very adaptable, one even being used to make snow for the film industry!

Throughout medieval times the Cotswold landscape was one of great spaciousness, with vast sheep walks alternating with common arable fields of several hundred acres. Arable farming methods produced distinct corrugations in the surface of the land, which resulted from repeated ploughing. Known as 'ridge and furrow', these landscape features can still be seen in some Cotswold fields and remain the most extensive form of surviving medieval archaeology.

The present landscape was defined by the Enclosure Acts between 1700 and 1840, when at least 120,000 acres of open land were enclosed by act of parliament. Without a ready supply of wood to build fences, and the soil too poor to cultivate hedgerows, it was the now familiar dry-stone wall which divided up the newly enclosed land for sheep. Enclosure in turn caused two major changes to the area. Firstly the landscape looked completely different as there were no longer large open spaces, and secondly, intensive sheep farming required fewer workers. This, combined with the movement of cloth manufacture away from the Cotswold cottage to the industrialised mill, caused the villages to depopulate, as workers left for the towns to seek work.

The Cotswolds became a sparsely populated rural backwater and many of its buildings fell into neglect. Industry did not move in as it was uneconomic to do so, hence the countryside remained unaltered. It wasn't until the arrival of the motor car in the 20th century, that the Cotswolds was opened up to tourists and those looking to escape from the towns.

Changes that occur now are less obvious. Rural and beautiful, the Cotswolds are less than two hours from London and property prices reflect this. That lovingly restored old weavers cottage you just walked past could be a second home used only at weekends. Nobody uses the village shop during the week and school rolls are falling. Thankfully the larger villages and towns still have their 'wool' churches, market places and fine buildings as reminders of the indigenous prosperity of bygone days.

Safety in the countryside

Road walking calls for particular care. When there is no defined footpath or wide verge, it is best to walk on the right so you are facing oncoming traffic. An exception would be a tight right hand bend where you should cross to the left in good time to improve your visibility.

Pushchairs. In order to cater for pushchairs some routes have used minor roads. Take the precaution of wearing bright clothes to improve your visibility to traffic.

Take a small first aid kit with you, even if it just consists of some antiseptic cream and a few plasters.

Refreshments, particularly water, can be vital towards the end of a walk on a warm summer's day.

All routes follow legitimate rights of way, but if you encounter an access problem and you are sure you are on a public right of way, then few landowners would object to you making a detour to get round the problem (although strictly speaking you would then be trespassing!). In the unlikely event that you find crops growing across a path, then common sense should prevail. It seems perfectly sensible, and more comfortable, to use the field margin to avoid damaging the crop. When you get home, the obstruction can then be reported to the Rights of Way Officer of the relevant County Council in order for the issue to be resolved. Nowadays this can be done on-line.

It is courteous to close gates after passing through, sometimes even if the gate was open when you arrived. Particularly if it is obvious that livestock may escape.

Mutual respect for farm animals is to be encouraged. Don't frighten or annoy them, but equally don't put you or your children in danger or discomfort. You certainly would not be the first walkers to go round the outside of a field of frisky bullocks. Cows are naturally curious and may approach you. They are also quite nervous and a clap of your hands will usually send them away. Never walk too close the back of a large animal because if you startle them they may kick out with their back legs.

Dogs should **ALWAYS** be kept on a lead anywhere near farm animals, and under close supervision elsewhere in the countryside.

The Countryside Code:

- Enjoy the countryside and respect its life and work.
- Guard against all risk of fire.
- Keep dogs under close control.
- Leave gates and property as you find them.

- Keep to public paths across farmland.
- Use gates and stiles to cross fences, hedges and walls.
- Leave livestock, crops and machinery alone.
- Help to keep all water clean.
- Protect plants and animals, and take your litter home.
- Take special care on country roads.
- Make no unnecessary noise - consider other people.
- Be safe - plan ahead and follow any signs.

Maps

Walks in this book are all contained within the area covered by Ordnance Survey Explorer Maps OL45, 168 and 179. These maps should be used to supplement the one given in the text.

A grid reference is given for the starting point of each walk. The first three digits are 'eastings' and correspond to the numbers along the bottom edge of the map, while the second three are 'northings', corresponding to the numbers along the map's vertical edge.

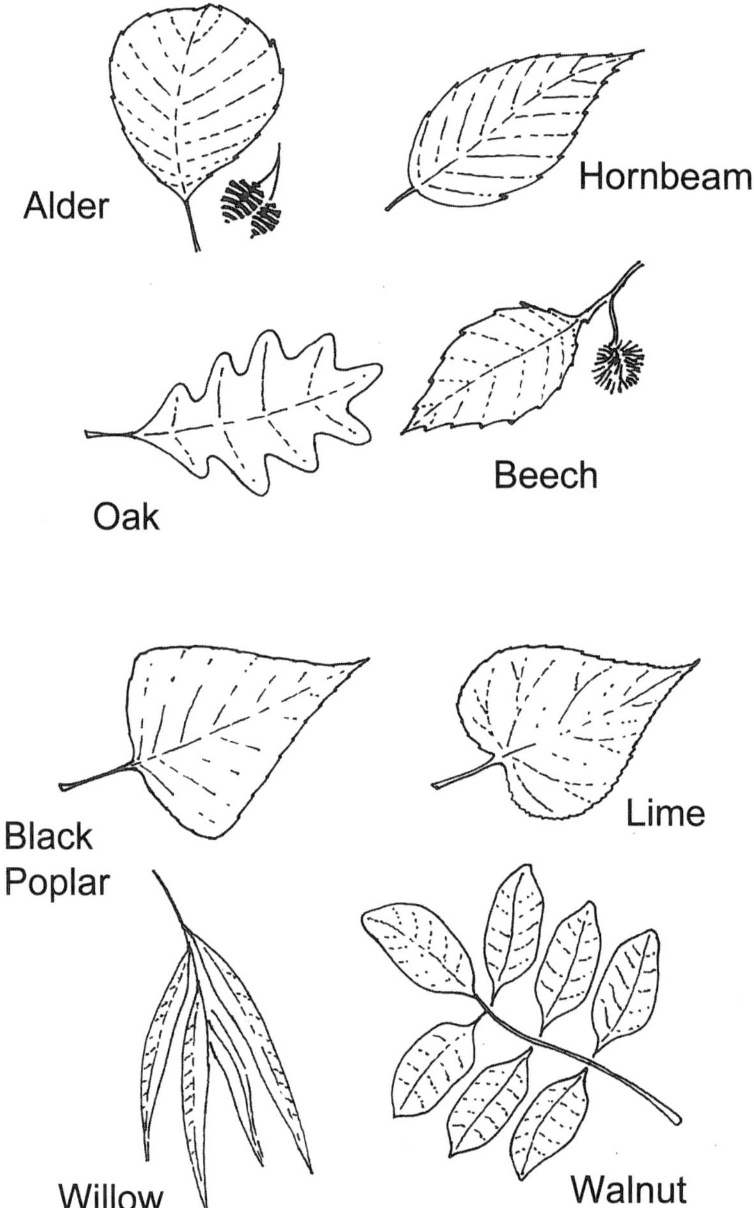
Alder
Hornbeam
Oak
Beech
Black
Poplar
Lime
Willow
Walnut

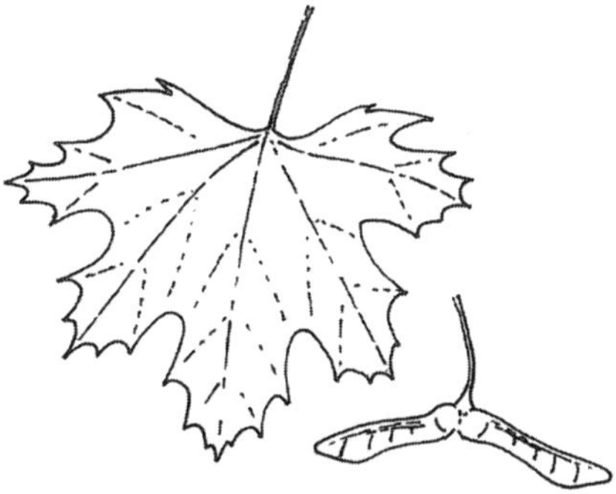

Norway Maple

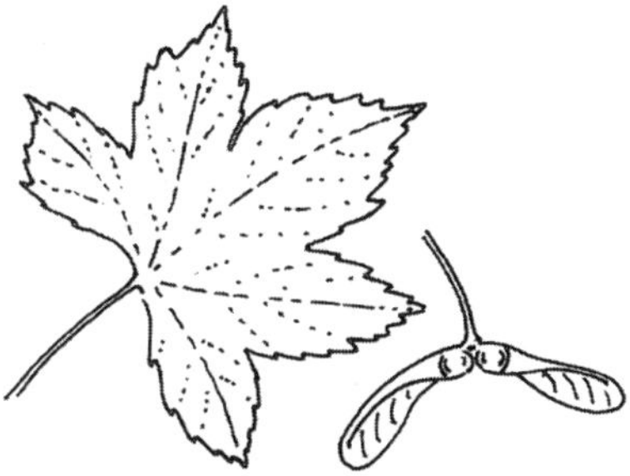

Sycamore

Field Maple

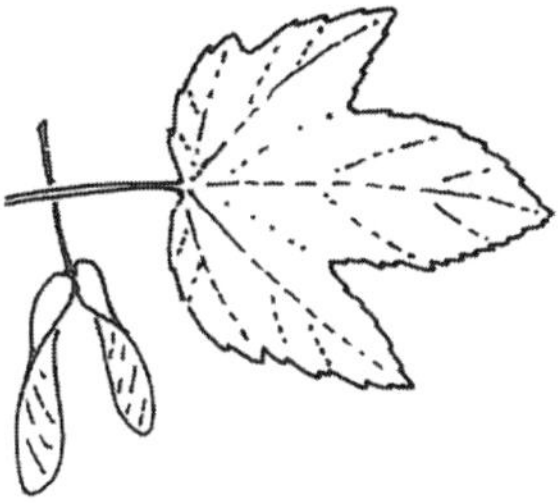

Red Maple

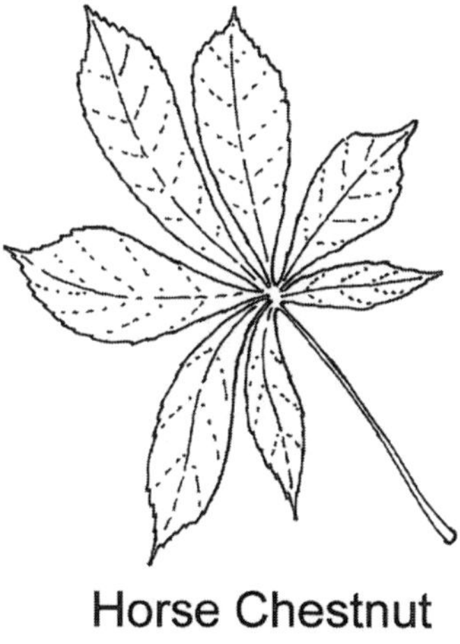

Horse Chestnut

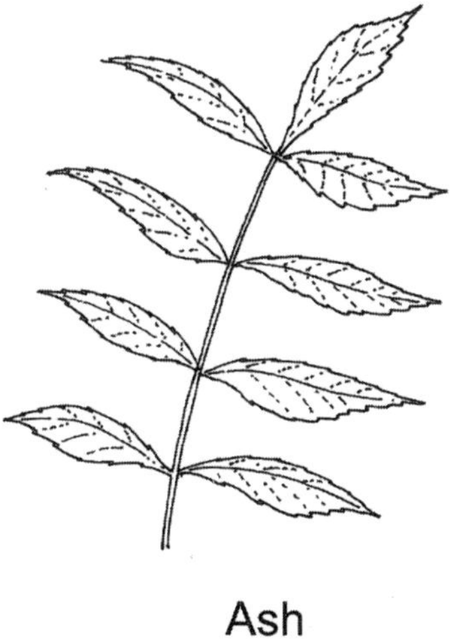

Ash

Walk 1. Blockley

Something for everyone: panoramic views, sylvan woodland, fast flowing streams and charming Cotswold mills. There's even a ford, the longest in the Cotswolds, so come prepared for a paddle!

Distance	5km (3 miles)
Starting point	Blockley is 4 miles north-west of Moreton-in-Marsh. Look for the B4479 which leaves the north side of the village to head for Paxford. From here, turn onto a road which heads east, signposted Draycott Village and Aston Magna. Park almost immediately on the left hand side of the road. Grid Reference: 167352 Postcode: GL56 9DB
Short cut	The easiest way to shorten the walk is to turn back when you reach Woolstaplers – see text
Terrain	Hilly walk along woodland tracks, fields and minor roads
Public toilets	Next to the village shop
Refreshments	Village shop and two pubs
Pushchairs	The route beyond the village is not suitable so use the short cut
Leaf collection	Sycamore, lime, beech and walnut
Map	OS Explorer Map OL45

Blockley

Blockley is a sparkling Cotswold gem, noted for its former silk mills which brought wealth and prosperity to the village during the 18th and 19th centuries. These were mostly driven by the powerful Blockley Brook, and at its peak there were eight silk mills employing 600 people, many of them children. At this time the population was nearly twice its present level and terraces of cottages were built up the hillside to accommodate the mill workers. There were seven pubs, three places of worship and a stately home nearby at Northwick Park, home to Lord and Lady Northwick. After the First World War Blockley's water driven mills ceased to be commercially viable, and within a decade, they had all been converted to private houses. The legacy of this industrial past is a wonderful mix of mills, workers cottages, almshouses and Georgian terraces, all clothed in the golden Cotswold Stone so typical of the area. Later, the fast flowing Blockley Brook enabled the village to become one of the first in the country to produce its own electricity.

Blockley remains a thriving community, and nowhere is this more apparent than in the local shop, which is run by volunteers as a co-operative.

The ford at Blockley

The walk

(*There are a few stiles early in the walk. If you have a pushchair it would be best to walk back up to the road junction, turn left, and follow the pavement to the pub where you can pick up the directions where shown* **.)

Walk down the road, passing the side entrance to 'The Old Silk Mill' before turning right onto a footpath opposite 'The Dell'. This mill, one of the largest in the village, is now largely hidden behind a screen of conifers. Cross a stile next to a five bar gate, and then another stile and footbridge before arriving at a junction of paths. Go straight on through a wooden gate, and soon you reach another of Blockley's old mills at the end of a narrow lane. Follow this up into the village and turn left into Station Road.

** Continue along to the Great Western Inn, where the former Westmacott Mill is visible at the bottom of the car park. This is now Blockley Court, a residential complex.

✓This building was a mill, a kind of factory which made silk in Victorian times. There were seven others in the village, and many of the workers were children who worked up to 50 hours a week. In 1845 a law was passed which meant that children had to be at least 8 years old to work in the mill. It wasn't all bad though. Most of the cottages in the village were cold to live in, but the mill had to be heated in order to make silk, so at least you were warm at work!

At the top of the hill, continue on into Lower Street, ignoring a turning high on the right which leads to the village centre. Walk beyond some **lime** trees, to reach Colebrook Cottage on the left.

✓This was once the village police station.
Q1 Can you see when it was built? (Clue: look up near the roof.)

Continue on to see Lower Terrace on your right.

✓Lower Terrace was built for the mill workers to live in.

Q2 Now you've got the hang of this, when was this building built?

Take care for the next 200m, because the road bends left and right and there is no pavement.

When the road straightens out, look to the left for a footpath (Quiet Lanes footpath) which follows the road up the hill (ignore the footpath to the left). After about 150m, turn right into School Lane. Soon you pass the entrance to Mill Dene, another of the village's former mills. It's hard to believe that this building was once the Vulcan Iron Foundry, producing, along with many other things, iron road gratings.

✓This was once a factory but is now a garden open to the public. There is a sign by the entrance.

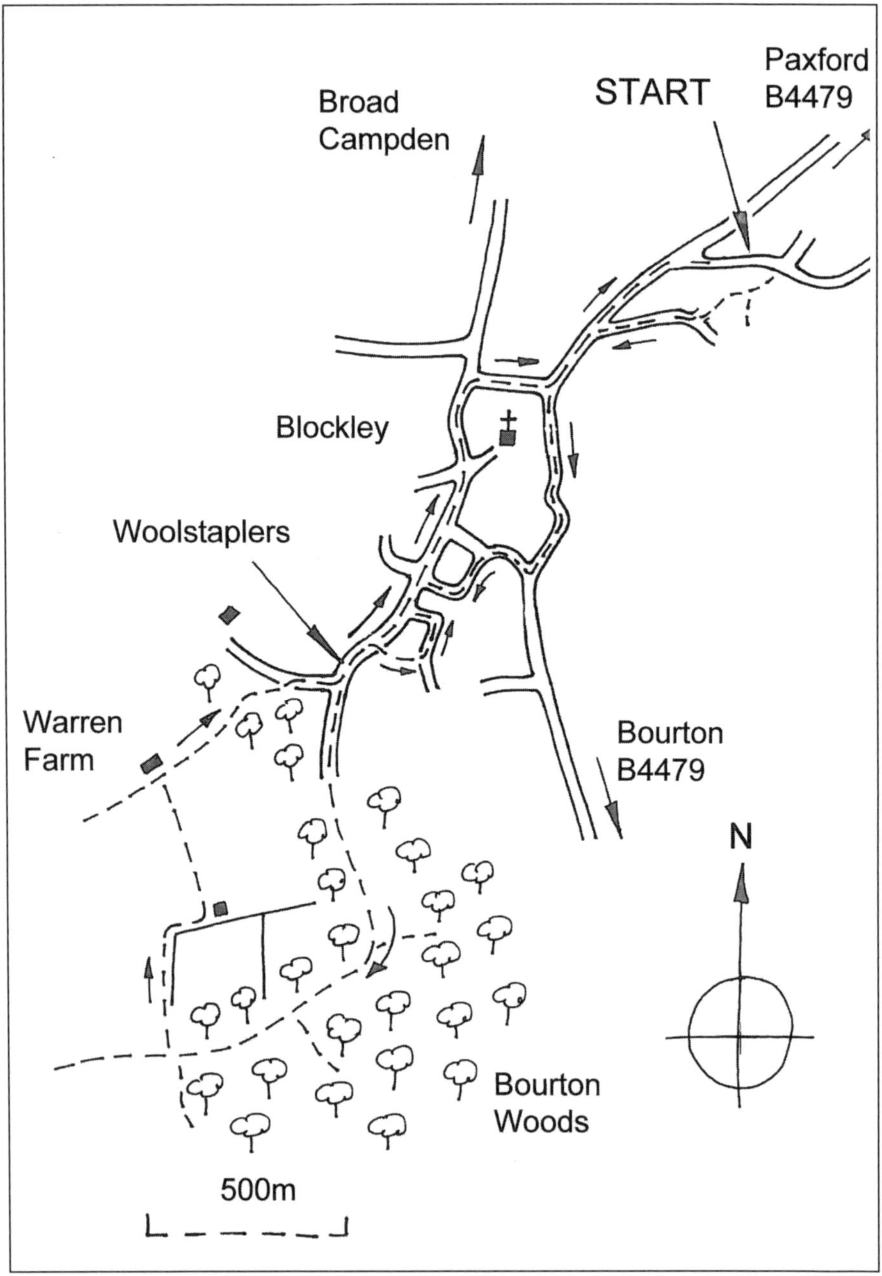

Paxford
B4479
START
Broad
Campden
Blockley
Woolstaplers
Warren
Farm
Bourton
B4479
N
Bourton
Woods
500m

Q3 Apart from deaf cats and daft ducks what else do you have to watch out for?

Fork left at the next junction onto a road marked 'unsuitable for motors'. This follows the Blockley Brook to another old mill before bending right and climbing up to the High Street.

Turn left here and walk along the raised pavement. After this finishes, continue along the road which bends left near 'Woolstaplers'. (*The walk can be shortened by turning back here and picking up the directions again where marked* *.)

Stay with the road as it passes Dovedale, once the highest mill on the Blockley Brook. Soon the road becomes a track, and after passing through a five-bar gate, you enter Bourton Woods.

Look down through the trees on the left for the many reservoirs which were created to help power the mills. The path now climbs through an area of mixed woodland.

✓ This wood is dark and mysterious. It may be quiet but there are eyes watching you. Squirrels, rabbits and pheasants are keeping still and waiting for you to pass by before they move again. The wood contains a mixture of broadleaf trees and conifers.

Broadleaf trees get their name because their leaves are broad and flat, unlike the conifers which have needle-like leaves. Conifers shed their leaves all year round and new ones grow all the time so they are never bare. As you pass them, see if you can tell which are broad-leafed and which are conifers. The conifers are often planted close together and compete with each other for sunlight. This makes them grow tall and straight.

Look at how dry the ground is under the conifers. They need a lot of water, and when they are planted this close together the ground becomes very dry. See if you can find both a **sycamore** and a **beech** leaf. Sycamore wood is used for kitchenware like chopping boards and wooden spoons.

After about 1000m, turn right onto a path which climbs up to a high kissing gate.

Q4 When should dogs be kept on a lead?

Continue straight ahead along a leafy path between two fields. Soon you are accompanied by a wire fence which you stay with as it turns right to head for an old barn. After 100m, turn left onto a track which heads towards the roof of a nearby farm.

Q5 How many triangular windows are there in the barn next to the farm?

Turn right at the farm and follow the track as it drops down the side of a field. Eventually you pass through some **walnut** trees to enter some woodland.

At the bottom of the wood, turn right onto a lane, and walk over a cattle-grid to reach a road junction. Turn left here, and follow the road as it bends right to pass 'Woolstaplers'.

* Turn right immediately after 'Woolstaplers' and find a narrow path which passes in front of 'Holland Cottage'.

Q6 How many cockrells are there on the gates?

Turn left when you reach an old track and walk down to the ford, the longest in the Cotswolds! Beyond the ford turn left, and walk back up into the village. Turn right at the High Street and keep to the right of the road, ignoring the raised pavement on the left.

Look out for the Russell Spring on the other side of the road.

✓This was built for the village by Lucy Russell and was once the main source of clean water at this end of the village. If you lived here in Victorian times, your first job after you got up in the morning was to fetch some water in a bucket. This would be used for drinking and washing. You might meet your friends here doing the same thing! Lucy ran the Malvern Mill, which is behind you at the back of 'The Stonehouse'.

It was very unusual for a woman to be in charge of a mill, but she was brave and clever, and proved to be better than most of the male mill owners. The silk trade collapsed in 1870, and her mill was then used to crush apples to make cider. There was always a smell of rotten apples at this end of the village!

Q7 Fill in the missing word: "Water from the Living Rock, Gods Precious Gift To ___".

Continue past the Crown Inn and pick up the raised pavement. Soon the church is visible on the right. You need to go slightly left here into Bell Lane, but before you do, cross the road and walk down to the churchyard entrance. If you still can't believe Blockley was ever industrial, look at the iron grating by the churchyard gate.

✓Look carefully at the grating. It was made at the Vulcan Iron Works which is now Mill Dene, the pretty garden you saw earlier in the walk. The owner of the iron works had his name cast into the grating.

Q8 What is his name?

Go back the way you came and turn right into Bell Lane. After passing the Almshouses you reach the village shop. This was originally built by Lady Northwick to house her carriage and horses while she attended church. There's another locally made grate nearby.

Continue past the Lime trees and pause by the bus shelter.

✓Look into the bus shelter. It was built when Princess Elizabeth was crowned Queen.

Q9 What year did she become Queen?

Turn right into St Georges Terrace and then left into Station Road. Pass the Great Western Inn again, and stay with the road now to Draycott Road and the start of the walk.

Blockley Checklist

- ☐ Stone ball
- ☐ Swings
- ☐ A door half way up a wall
- ☐ Wheely bin
- ☐ Duck
- ☐ Sheep
- ☐ Red telephone box
- ☐ Cattle grid
- ☐ Someone playing bowls

Walk 2. Winchcombe

A walk with something for everyone. An ancient Saxon town, some quiet riverside meadows and the landscaped parkland of a medieval castle.

Distance	**5km (3 miles)**
Starting point	**Back Lane car park. This lies on the west side of the town and is easily reached from North Street (B4078). Turn into Back Lane and you'll find the car park behind the Library. Grid Reference: 023284 Postcode: GL54 5PZ**
Short cut	**Yes. See text and dotted line on map**
Terrain	**A level walk along pavements, grassy paths and estate tracks**
Public toilets	**At the car park**
Refreshments	**Many pubs and tea shops in the town**
Pushchairs	**The route is suitable for pushchairs provided the weather has been dry for a few days. There are three kissing gates**
Leaf collection	**Hornbeam and horse chestnut**
Map	**OS Explorer Map OL45**

Winchcombe

Winchcombe is not like other Cotswold towns. It has its own river, its own saint, was a king's capital and a centre of pilgrimage. It had an Abbey, a royal castle, and in Saxon times was the most important town in the Cotswolds. The Abbey may have gone but the castle remains, and St Peter's church, with its gargoyles and pinnacles, towers over the elegant houses and picturesque cottages gathered around it.

Sudeley Castle

Bound up with the history of the town is Sudeley Castle, which has many royal connections. Henry VIII, Elizabeth I, Catherine of Aragon, Catherine Parr and Charles I all spent time here.

The Gatehouse at Sudeley Castle

The Castle dates back to 1140 but was largely rebuilt in the 15th century and made into a Tudor country estate. It was ruined in the civil war when its roof was removed, leaving it at the mercy of the elements. For 200 years the castle and chapel were left to rot and local people used its stone for their own building projects. King George II visited Sudeley in 1788 to see the ruins – and fell down a flight of stairs. He was only saved from serious injury by the housekeeper who broke his fall.

Queen Elizabeth I left a christening robe, Katherine of Aragon an altar cloth and Catherine Parr a ghost, but the woman who made the biggest impression on the town was Emma Dent. In 1855, she and her husband inherited the castle from wealthy Worcester glove-makers, John and William Dent, who had begun the re-construction in 1837. Over the next 45 years, she threw herself enthusiastically into completing the castle's restoration, filling the interior with fine art and objects associated with the long history of the estate. She was also a generous benefactor to the town, building the school and the almshouses that bear her name. The initials 'E.D.' crop up many times on this walk!

The Walk

Head into the corner of the car park (sign-posted Town Centre) and turn right into Cowl Lane.

This soon takes you to the High Street where you turn left. Soon you turn left again into North Street but before you do, pause by the Police Museum and the stocks.

✓A long time ago these were used to punish criminals. They would have their legs or wrists fitted through the round holes and locked in place. They wouldn't be able to get away and could be left here for days. Is this worse than the 'naughty step'?

Q1 How many holes are there in the stocks?

Proceed along North Street.

✓Many years ago, horses were bought and sold along this street. To stop them running away, they would be tied to metal rings fixed to the wall. The last shop before Bull Lane (Pheonix Bookshop) has one near the door. Soon you will pass 22 North St (currently the Co-Op).

Q2 How many rings can you see outside this shop?

Turn right into Chandos Street. At the end of Chandos Street turn left onto the Broadway Road (B4632). Cross the road at a convenient point and follow the road as it bends right to reach the bridge over the River Isbourne.

Q3 When was the bridge built? (Clue: look at the plaque on the wall.)

Immediately after the bridge, turn right to find a kissing gate, which leads to a riverside pasture. Follow the path over two bridges, to reach a third field being used as a paddock.

✓Towards the end of this field you can see a water trough. In summer a horse can drink almost a bath-full of water every day!

Pass through a kissing gate and walk beside some cottages to reach a road. Turn left here, and walk up the leafy lane to reach the gatehouse of Sudeley Castle. This was built by Emma Dent in Victorian times as part of the restoration of the castle. Look up at the window above the archway.

✓The letters E.D. stand for Emma Dent. At one time the castle was just a ruin but she helped re-build it. The words are in Latin, a very old language which isn't

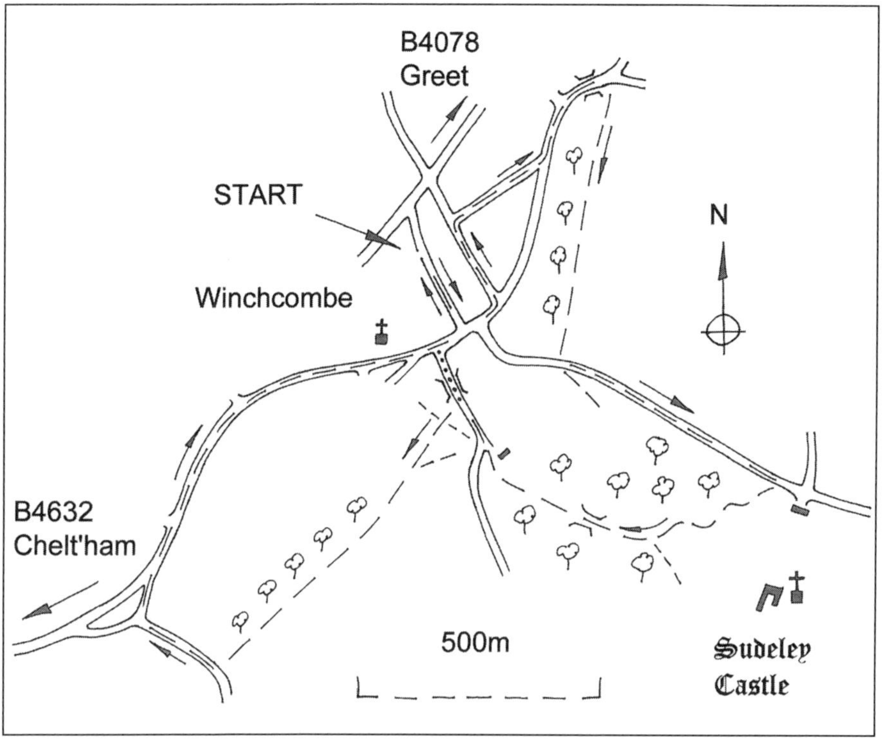

used much now. The words mean: 'to friends, any hour you please'. Emma is sending her friends a sort of coded message, asking them to visit whenever they liked.

Q4 When was this built?

Go back the way you came and follow the wall round to the left to reach the castle entrance. Walk through the gate and keep to the left as you enter the gravelled car park. Soon you get a glimpse of the castle over to the left.

Catherine Parr, the last surviving wife of Henry VIII, came to Sudeley in 1548, but her brief stay ended in tragedy the following year when she died during childbirth. The child survived however, but the ghost of Catherine is said to haunt the castle looking for the daughter she never knew. Mementoes of Catherine Parr still survive at Sudeley, including a portrait and a love letter written by her to Thomas Seymour. She rests below a marble tomb in the lovely chapel that bears her name.

✓Henry VIII married six times. His last wife, Katherine Parr, lived here for a while. Her ghost has been seen at one of the windows wearing a long green dress!

Q5 Can you think of another royal Catherine?

Follow the trellis fence round the visitor centre, and then turn right to find a tarmac driveway accompanied by a fence. This soon turns left to go through the parkland. After passing to the left of a **hornbeam**, it bends right near a **horse chestnut** and descends gently down to an elegant stone bridge bearing the tell-tale initials.

✓Can you see any ducks in the lake below? Ducks and Geese 'moult' in summer which means that some of their feathers fall out helping them keep cool in the hot weather. Look out for their feathers in the grass. The feathers grow back as the weather gets colder.

Q6 When was the bridge built? (Clue: look at the wall of the bridge about half way across.)

Pass the gate house to reach a minor road where you go straight ahead towards the town. Just before the stone bridge, turn left and walk through a kissing gate to reach a meadow.

(*To use the short cut, go straight on here across the bridge and climb up to a road junction. Turn right here and pick up the direction again where shown* *).

After about 100m, look over your right shoulder for a view of the church rising up above the town.

Q7 What kind of animal stands on top of the church spire?

Continue straight on, along a path which rises gently up to a gate. Follow the path beyond to a lane where you turn right. Walk down the lane and turn right at the road junction. This was the old road between Winchcombe and Cheltenham before the current re-alignment was built a little to the west.

Walk past an ivy covered cottage and a pause by the post box.

✓Can you see that the post box has the letters GR on it? This stands for George Rex, which means that this post box was made when King George was on the throne.

Q8 Most post boxes now have ER on them. What do you think the E stands for?

Turn right at the main road and walk into the town. As you approach the Corner Cupboard Inn look right for Rabbit Box House.

✓ A long time ago, a family with 13 children lived here! At this time water wasn't supplied into your home like it is now. To have a bath you had to fetch the water from a well in a bucket, and then heat it over the fire. It was then poured into a tub, and the whole family took turns to have a bath in the same water! The water was very dirty when the last child got in the tub. It was so much effort you might only have a bath every 6 months!

Q9 What kind of animal can be found above the door?

✓The pub is haunted by the ghost of a 12 year old girl so stay on this side of the road!

Just beyond Cotswold House pause by No 42, which has a metal plaque on the wall with a sun on it.

Before municipal fire brigades were formed, they were operated by the Insurance Companies. This house was originally insured by the Sun Insurance company, who placed this Fire Mark on the outside of the insured property to guide their fire brigade. The Sun Company was established in 1710 and still exists today as Royal & Sun Alliance. It's the oldest insurance company still bearing its original name.

Just before the church, cross the road near 'Three Gables' and head for a small courtyard. The building with the two gabled ends is the old school with the tell-tale initials 'E.D.'.

Q10 When was the school built? (Clue: look up near the roof)

Pass the 'Teacher's House' and pause by the church of St. Peter which has an excellent collection of gargoyles, one of which is said to be the model for Lewis Carroll's Mad Hatter.

Beyond the church, look right down pretty Vineyard Street with its avenue of limes.

* Across the road, just before the Plaisterer's Arms are the Dent Almshouses. No prizes for guessing who built these!

Where the road narrows, turn left into Cowl Lane and return to the car park and the start of the walk.

Winchcombe Checklist

☐ Round window	☐ Stone ball
☐ Clock	☐ Horse
☐ Horse shoe	☐ Duck
☐ Bell	☐ A man walking a dog
☐ Post box	☐ Satellite dish

Walk 3. The Slaughters

A delightful walk around two villages collectively known as 'The Slaughters'. There are clear shallow streams, pretty stone footbridges, honey coloured cottages and plenty of opportunities for little feet to splash around, so come prepared! The Slaughters' quintessential English charm make them a honey pot for tourists, but without the hustle and bustle of nearby Bourton-on-the-Water.

Distance	5km (3 miles)
Starting point	Just north of the Coach and Horses Inn on the A429 Fosse Way is Meadow Way/Beddome Way, which leads into Bourton Industrial Park. Leave the A429 here, and turn immediately left into a cul-de-sac, where a car may be left. Grid Reference: 170219 Postcode: GL54 2HQ
Short cut	The old mill in Lower Slaughter would be a convenient place to cut the walk short – see text
Terrain	A level walk along well used footpaths and minor roads. There is a busy road that will have to be crossed with care
Public toilets	Only those available to patrons of the Coach and Horses Inn
Refreshments	The Coach and Horses Inn
Pushchairs	The route is suitable for pushchairs provided the weather has been dry for a few days. There are four kissing gates between Lower and Upper Slaughter, three of which are repeated on the return journey
Leaf collection	Oak, ash and lime
Map	OS Explorer Map OL45

The Slaughters

Lower Slaughter is centred on an old water mill and a former manor house, which was a convent until the dissolution of the monasteries in 1553. The only surviving link with the Manor's monastic past is the convent's 14th century dovecote, which still stands in the grounds of the manor, now a hotel. The building you see today dates back to 1655, and was largely the creation of celebrated stonemason Valentine Strong. The 13th century Parish Church of St. Mary was rebuilt in 1867. The mill was last used commercially in the 1960s and now houses a museum/craft centre.

The building that dominates Upper Slaughter is the beautiful gabled Manor House, which was once a rectory but now a hotel. The oldest part of the house dates from the 15th century but the front is Elizabethan. The medieval almshouses around the village square were reconstructed in 1906 under the direction of Sir Edward Lutyens, and to complete the picture there's the Old School House, a tiny Chapel, a Village Hall and the Parish Church of St Peter. The only thing you won't see is a war memorial, Upper Slaughter being one of the few 'thankful villages' whose servicemen all returned safely from both world wars.

The walk

Walk back to the main road and after turning left you reach the Coach and Horses Inn.

The Old Mill Lower Slaughter

✓Before the motor car and the train, the only means of travelling between distant places was a coach pulled by horses. The building at the end of the car park was once a stable where fresh horses would be kept to replace the tired ones which had pulled the coach from Cheltenham. It was a cold and bumpy ride because the roads were poor and sometimes you would have to get out on a steep hill to make it easier for the horses. Horses would be changed every 10-15 miles and from here it might take 10 hours to reach London. How far would you get if you travelled for 10 hours now?

Q1 Look at the pub sign - how many horses are pulling the coach? (Look carefully!)

Cross the road and take a footpath sign-posted 'Heart of England Way' (it may be safer to cross the road at the traffic light controlled junction further down). Follow this well made path as it passes to the right of a paddock.

✓The large hedgerow on the right contains a number of common shrubs such as hawthorn (red berries), sloe (mauve), elder (small purple berries), bramble and ivy. They provide shelter for a number of small wild animals and nesting sites for birds.

Eventually the path crosses the River Eye which now accompanies you into Lower Slaughter. Follow the stream round to the left near Lower Slaughter Manor and look to the right to see the distant parish church.

Q2 What sits on top of the church spire?

Pause by a bridge which carries the road over the river.

✓The tree on the other side of the road with its distinctive hanging branches is a willow tree. In ancient times the bark of the willow was crushed down to a powder and used to relieve aches and pains. They found the magic ingredient and used it to develop modern painkillers like Aspirin.

Cross the road here and go straight on, keeping the river on your left. Soon you pass the village green with its gabled fountain, erected by the Lord of the Manor, Charles S. Whitmore, in Victorian times.

Q3 The water comes out of an animal's mouth. What sort of animal it is?
Q4 When was it built? (Clue: look up.)

Continue along the path and soon you pass the gate of Vine cottage.

✓There is an old metal sign on the cottage gate. This sign was originally fitted to a gate near a railway. It is important that gates near railways are kept shut to stop farm animals from getting onto the line and causing accidents.

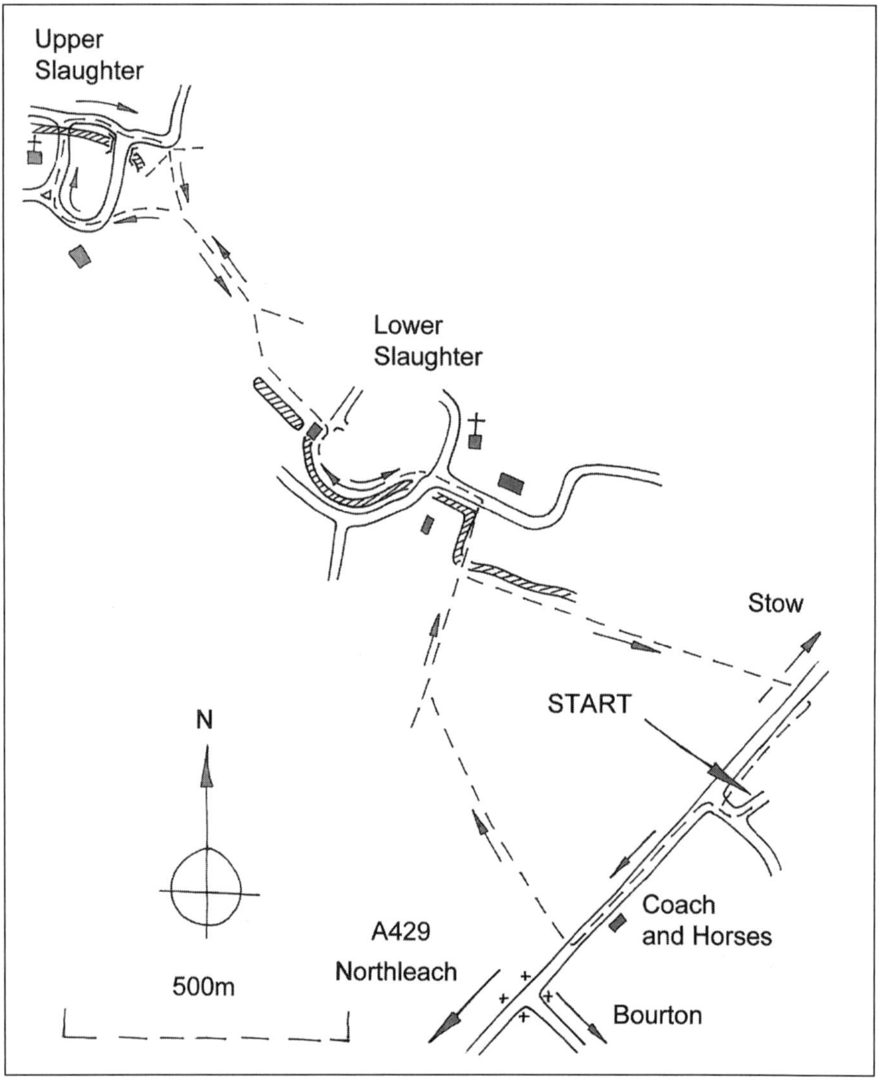

Q5 How much was the fine?

Follow the river through the village until you come to the old mill with its brick built chimney and water wheel. (*This would be a convenient place to shorten the walk. Go back the way you came and pick up the directions again where shown* *.)

✓As you pass the mill look at the post box in the wall. It has the letters GR on it. This stands for George Rex which means that this post box was made when King George was on the throne. Older post boxes might have VR on them which means they were made when Victoria was Queen.

Q6 Most post boxes now have ER on them. What do you think the E stands for?

Turn left immediately after the mill onto a footpath which passes through two gates before leaving the village behind. The second gate was made in the year that Prince Charles, our future King, married Lady Diana.

Q7 what year did they get married?

✓The water on the left was a reservoir for the mill. It stored water during periods of heavy rain so that in drier times there would be enough water to drive the mill wheel. This would be fixed to a mill stone which crushed corn to make flour. Later the mill was powered by a steam engine and they built the chimney to take the smoke away.

After passing through a gate you follow an obvious path across a meadow. Pass through a kissing gate on the far side and continue along a well used path across a second, longer meadow to reach another gate at the far side shaded by an **oak** tree. After going straight on, look to the right - you will be returning from this direction later.

The appearance of the Lords of the Manor Hotel across the valley on the left heralds your imminent arrival at Upper Slaughter. The path soon drops down to another gate and after crossing a stone bridge, it climbs up to a road. Turn left here, and follow the road round to the right, passing an old water pump on the left.

✓Water is now piped into our homes from reservoirs and you can turn it on with a tap. If you lived in this village in Victorian times, you and your mother would walk from your cottage to this pump to fetch some water for drinking and washing. The pump once had a long handle which was pulled up and down to make water come out of the spout. The water comes from a spring in the ground below. Some people were sad when 'tap water' arrived here about 60 years ago because they liked to meet their friends here for a chat. Look out for another pump later on.

Soon you arrive at the triangular village green of Upper Slaughter with its two trees, an **ash** and a **lime**. Bear right here, but before you do, wander over to the green and rest for a moment on the bench, which was placed here in memory of Agnes Witts.

✓Twenty five of the villagers went off to fight in the First World War and one of these was Agnes. Most women helped to nurse the wounded soldiers but Agnes wanted to do more and became a driver in the army. This was very unusual at the time. What was more unusual was that all twenty five of them returned safely back to the village.

Q8 How old was Agnes when she died?

Leave the village green and head in the direction of the distant telephone box. Just beyond this is the village school which is now a private residence. Look carefully at it and you will still see the school bell high up on the wall.

✓ In 1932 there were 19 children attending this school and they were all taught together in the same classroom. Imagine being in the same class as your brother or sister!

Q9 In what year was the school built? (Clue: look up near the roof.)

Follow the road down to a ford – surely one of the Cotswolds' most idyllic spots. You can cross using the stone pedestrian bridge or take your shoes off and paddle. Look left for another bridge further upstream and a row of honey-coloured cottages where time seems to have stood still. Follow the road round to the right until you arrive at a road junction. (Note the water pump on the right.)

Turn left here and follow the lane up-hill until, as it bends left, you see a metal farm gate on the right. Ignore the obvious path beyond the gate and instead bear right, taking a path that passes to the left of a power line support. After crossing this short meadow you reach the gate you walked through earlier. Pass through this gate and re-trace your route back to the Mill Museum.

* From the museum, follow the river back through the village, staying with it as it turns right near the entrance to Lower Slaughter Manor. Cross the bridge over the river again but instead of re-tracing your steps, turn left immediately after the bridge to follow the riverside path. (*There are three kissing gates and a stile on this section so pushchairs might prefer to go straight on, retracing the route back to the start.*)

✓As you walk alongside the brook look out for the hairy broad leaves and bell shaped pink flowers of the comfrey. They love damp places and were once used to help heal broken bones and severe burns as well as many other illnesses.

Continue along the river bank to reach the busy A429 Fosse Way. This lies immediately beyond the last gate so take care as you approach. Cross the stile on the other side of the road and turn right, following the path which runs parallel with the nearby road to reach the start of the walk.

The Slaughters Checklist

☐ Horse	☐ Fallen tree
☐ Stone ball	☐ Bell
☐ Duck	☐ Red telephone box
☐ Horse shoe	☐ A road covered in water
☐ Witches broom stick	

Walk 4. Chalford

Secluded water-side paths, magnificent old mills, quaint hillside cottages and groceries delivered by Donkey! A short walk packed full of variety and interest. Directions have to be followed carefully along the donkey paths.

Distance	**5 km (3 miles)**
Starting point	**Chalford is 6 miles east of Stroud on the A419. Park east of the church in a lay-by alongside the A419. Grid Reference: 893025 Postcode: GL6 8PW**
Short cut	**Yes – see text**
Terrain	**The route is level but will require some care. The A419 is never far away and there are narrow lanes and canal-side paths. The steep section along the donkey path is optional**
Public toilets	**Only available to patrons of the New Red Lion**
Refreshments	**The New Red Lion Inn**
Pushchairs	**The route is suitable for pushchairs. There are no stiles or kissing gates but there is a flight of steps, and a boarded railway crossing**
Leaf collection	**Ash, sycamore, beech and lime**
Map	**OS Explorer Map 168**

The Chalford

Chalford is a beautiful and unique village, almost alpine in character, which clings to the steep sides of the Golden Valley. The village dates back to the boom years of the Cotswold cloth industry, when mills lined the valley floor, weaver's cottages clung precariously to the valley sides, and clothier's houses occupied the best locations. The weavers came looking for work from the 17th century onwards, and built themselves cottages on the steep hillside. Any situation would do, the more inaccessible the plot, the cheaper it was buy.

This made access difficult, and donkeys were used to move cloth and wool between the cottages and the mills. These cottages can still only be reached on foot.

The arrival of the Thames and Severn canal in 1789 brought more prosperity and larger mills to Chalford. Many of the surviving mills can be seen on this walk.

The weavers may have gone but Rack Hill, where they dried their cloth on racks, still survives.

The Chalford Donkeys

After the cloth trade disappeared, donkeys continued to be used to carry coal and household items up the steep 'donkey paths' until as recently as the 1950s.

Chalford's village shop, like many others, lost its struggle for survival against the car and the supermarket, but in 2003 it re-opened as a community shop staffed by volunteers. The donkey delivery service was re-introduced in 2008 to worldwide media interest.

The Donkeys are loaded up outside the Chalford Community Stores (tel: 01453 882288) between 7:30 and 8 am every Saturday morning, so an early start is essential if you want to see Teddy and Chester in action! The walk contains an optional extension that follows the donkey path up the hillside.

The shop is run by volunteers as a co-operative, so please patronise it so this old tradition can continue.

✓We are going to imagine what it was like to be a child here 200 years ago.

Home delivery Chalford style with Teddy the Donkey

The walk

Walk away from the Church to reach the triangle, where you fork left into 'High Street'. The village shop is ahead of you on the right. Continue past the shop to 'The Corner House', where you turn left onto a path that climbs up behind the house.

*(This optional route explores the donkey paths. There are a couple of steep hills and some steps to negotiate. This can be omitted – stay with the road and pick up directions again where shown *.)*

After a few metres turn sharp left, and after walking up some steps turn right. The path climbs gently up to another which soon appears over your left shoulder. Ignore this and continue along the level path to reach an obvious fork. You will be returning along the left fork, but for now go slightly right, following a path which is accompanied by a wooden railing. This soon reaches Apple Cottage.

✓If you lived in Apple Cottage 200 years ago, your whole family (yes that includes you!) would be working in the cottage six days a week, making cloth out of wool. It would be carried down to the mill (a kind of factory) on a donkey to be dyed and finished.

Go straight on past the cottage. Eventually the path climbs up to a road where you turn left. Across the road is the old Sunday school.

✓Sunday was your day off. You would have gone to this school for a couple of hours to learn how to read and write and do basic sums.

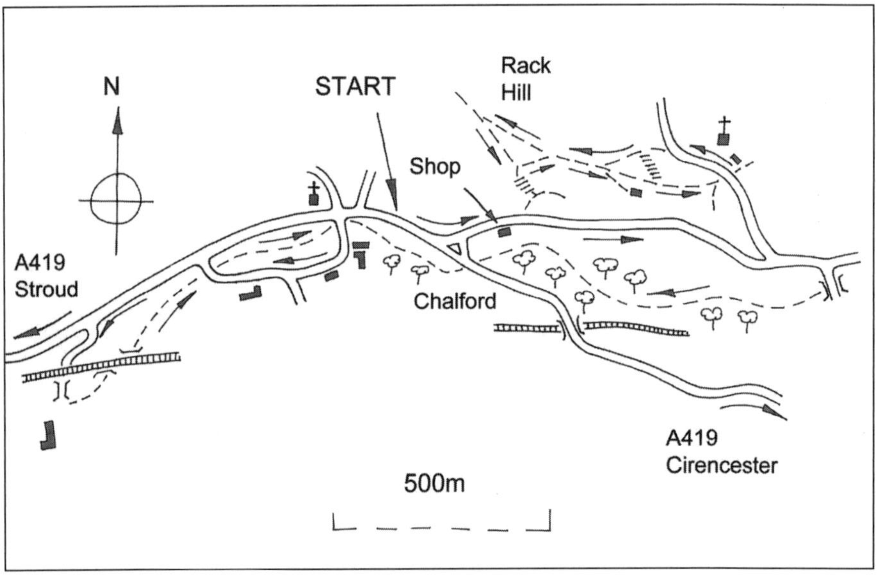

Continue up the hill past the Baptist Church, and turn left after 'The Rockery' onto a narrow lane signed as a cul-de-sac. After passing some roof tops the path returns you back to the fork you left earlier. Continue back the way you came and soon, where the path drops steeply left, continue straight on along a grassy path on a ledge. This soon reaches another path where you turn sharp left. Turn right at the bottom and right again at the bottom of the steps to reach the High Street, where you turn left.

* Continue along the High Street to reach the New Red Lion Inn.

Q1 When did the pub open? (Clue: look at the sign.)

Walk past the 'Seventh Day Adventist Hall'.

✓This was once a bakery. Now it's a kind of church.

Q2 Can you see when it became a church? (Clue: look above the window.)

Continue on to the Tankard Spring.

✓200 years ago water was not supplied to houses like it is now and you couldn't get it by just turning on a tap. As soon as you were strong enough to carry a bucket, you would be sent down here to get some water for drinking and washing. You might meet your friends at the spring doing the same thing.

The nearby cottages relied on this water source until the 1950s and there was no electricity or gas either!

Follow the road through the village, passing some new houses built on the site of Sevilles Mill. Sevilles Mill House and Bubblewell both date back over 400 years, and were once mill owner's houses. Soon you reach Coppice Hill, where you go straight on down the hill past 'Green Court' and 'The Mount', both former cloth merchant's houses.

Turn right at the bottom of the hill near a detached garage, and then right again onto a riverside path.

✓On your left is an old canal, a kind of man-made river. 200 years ago, the cloth you made at home with your parents might be transported in boats along the canal to places as far away as London, where it would be made into smart suits or uniforms. The old canal is now full of water plants like the yellow flag iris, which loves damp places.

All these cottages once had outside toilets which discharged straight into the river. Mains sewerage did not arrive until 1961.

Continue along the canal-side path which is shaded by **ash** and **sycamore**. Eventually you reach the A419 which is crossed to reach a car park on the other side. Re-gain the path near a power line and soon you are walking over the outstretched roots of **beech** trees which line the river at this point.

✓Roots take water to the tree and also food from the soil. They usually spread over a large area which helps the tree to stay upright. They spread out almost as far as the branches above you, but most are out of sight deep underground.

Can you see the empty shells of beech nuts on the ground? The nuts have been eaten by squirrels. When there are too many to eat, they will bury them for later in the year. Sometimes they forget where they buried them and the nuts remain in the soil to grow into new trees in the spring. Do you sometimes forget where you left things?

If you are quiet and look up into the trees you may see a grey squirrel running along the branches.

Q3 You are most likely to see a grey squirrel. What other squirrel lives in this country?

Shortly you reach the main road again near some tree stumps. Turn left here and follow the road down to the right as it passes the entrance to Chalford Industrial Estate. There were a total of six mills on this site, but now only the New, Mugmore and Bliss Mills remain. In late Victorian times, over 1,000 people were employed here making walking sticks.

Walk past Chalford Place to reach Belvedere Mill.

✓This is a mill, a kind of factory where wool was made into cloth. Wages were so low that the whole family (yes including you!) would have to work in the mill. Your family really needed the money you earned in here. It was nice and warm in the mill but it was noisy and dangerous. If you got your fingers trapped in the machine you would lose some of your pay, especially if you spilt blood on the cloth (this really happened). This was because they would have to stop the machine to clean it and throw away the blood-stained cloth.

Walk along the road to reach the A419 where you turn left. After walking past some **lime** trees, pause by Hampton Lane.

✓This road goes down to an old canal bridge which was only meant to carry a horse and cart. It's important that heavy lorries don't cause the bridge to collapse.

Q4 What is the weight limit on this bridge?

Continue with care along the main road until, where it bends right, you turn left onto a track which drops down to a level crossing. Cross the line quickly but carefully. Once you are beyond the gate look back at the warning sign.

Q5 What does it say? "Stop, Look, Listen, beware of……"

Turn left after the canal bridge to find a towpath at the bottom of a flight of steps. Before you do though, wander on for a few metres to see St Mary's, another of Chalford's old mills.

Return to the canal and walk up past the old lock to find a strange looking metal object stuck in the ground.

✓This was placed here in 1845 when the railway was built. It marks the boundary of the land owned by the railway.

Q6 What is the name of the Railway Company? "The Great…."

Eventually you climb up to a road. Go straight on here to find the path again just beyond a line of lock up garages.

Q7 How many garages are there?

Soon you pass a round house which was built around 1789 when the canal was opened.

✓In order to use the canal you had to pay a fee or toll. This was collected by a canal worker who lived in this house.

Follow the path up to a road. Across the road is Chalford Church.

Q8 Can you see what sort of animal is standing on the church tower?

Cross the road carefully and turn right to reach the start of the walk.

Chalford Checklist

- ☐ Round window
- ☐ Clcok
- ☐ Horse shoe
- ☐ A round house
- ☐ Satellite dish
- ☐ Waterfall
- ☐ Post box
- ☐ Duck

Walk 5. Cirencester

A walk which takes you through the splendour of Earl Bathurst's estate, elegant Cecily Hill and medieval Coxwell Street, to reach the magnificent old 'wool church' of St John the Baptist. There is much to see; regency terraces, quaint back streets, quiet riverside paths and possibly the world's tallest yew hedge!

The route passes through the Bathurst Estate, which is only open between 8am and 5pm so plan your day accordingly.

Distance	**5km (3 miles)**
Starting point	**Head for Cirencester's southern bypass, the A419. At the roundabout near the hospital, take the exit sign-posted town centre, coach park and superstore. Follow the directions to the leisure centre and its car park. Grid Reference: 018017 Postcode: GL7 1US**
Short cut	**One – see text and dotted line on map**
Terrain	**A flat walk over estate tracks, riverside paths and narrow pavements**
Public toilets	**There are toilets in the Abbey grounds behind the church**
Refreshments	**There are many tea shops and pubs in the town centre**
Pushchairs	**The route is suitable for pushchairs. There are no stiles or kissing gates**
Leaf collection	**Lime, horse chestnut, ash and sycamore**
Map	**OS Explorer Map OL45**

Cirencester

After London, Cirencester was the most important roman settlement in Britain. It began life as a fort on the Fosse Way, which for a few decades after the Roman invasion in 43AD, marked the western frontier of the occupied zone.

The native Dobunni tribe occupied a settlement of significant size nearby at Bagendon, but were not warlike people and readily adopted the Romano-

British lifestyle. In response, the Romans accepted many of the local customs and culture and this is reflected in the Roman name of the town, Corinium Dobunnorum.

When the frontier moved west following the conquest of Wales, a large forum and basilica was built over the site of the fort, and by the time the city wall was completed in the 2nd century it enclosed an area of 240 acres.

The Dobunni tribe eventually abandoned Bagendon, and adopted the town as their administrative centre. No doubt they shared the Roman enthusiasm for sports such as cock fighting and bear baiting because a large amphitheatre was built on the south side of the town in the 2nd century. Its substantial earthworks still exist and these can be found southeast of the hospital. Apart from this, few Roman remains now exist above ground level, but the Corinium Museum houses a splendid collection of artefacts including many Roman Mosaics.

Most of present day Cirencester dates back to the Middle Ages, except for the impressive Abbey of St Mary, which was destroyed during the Dissolution of the Monasteries in 1539.

Cirencester Park and Broad Ride from the church tower

The Walk

Turn left out of the car park and follow the high wall of Cirencester Park. As the main road joins from the left, look right for a gatehouse, which gives access to the park grounds. Beyond the gatehouse, walk straight on along a drive bordered with **lime** trees.

Eventually you arrive at a cross roads. The route continues right here along Broad Ride, which heads towards the distant church, but if time allows turn left and explore the parkland. Please remember you walk here as a privileged guest, and to take your litter home.

This was once the main road to Stroud until the early 19th century, when the third Earl Bathurst incorporated it into Cirencester Park. After constructing an alternative route nearby (now the A419) as compensation, he set about straightening the road and landscaping the area. The **horse chestnuts** which line the drive probably date back to this period.

At the end of the drive, walk through the gates into Cecily Hill. At the bottom, look across the street at the Tontine Building. This building is so named because it was the prize in a now illegal winner-takes-all financial scheme where, following the death of every other member, the last surviving participant wins the prize. In this case Earl Bathurst.

Q1 How old is this building? (Clue: look above the arch.)

At the end of Cecily Hill turn left into Thomas Street. (*You can short-cut here by turning right and then right again into Park Lane. Pick up the directions again where shown* *). Turn immediately right into Coxwell Street and begin a loop around one of the oldest parts of the town. At the bottom of Coxwell turn left and look up at the shop on the corner.

✓This used to be a music shop. Can you see the statues above the shop? One of them is playing an instrument.

Q2 How many statues are there?

After 150m turn left into Thomas Street.

✓The old wooden door at St Thomas' Hospital is over 500 years old. Can you see how worn the step is under the door? A lot of people have used this step!

After Thomas Street bends left, pause near an old post box.

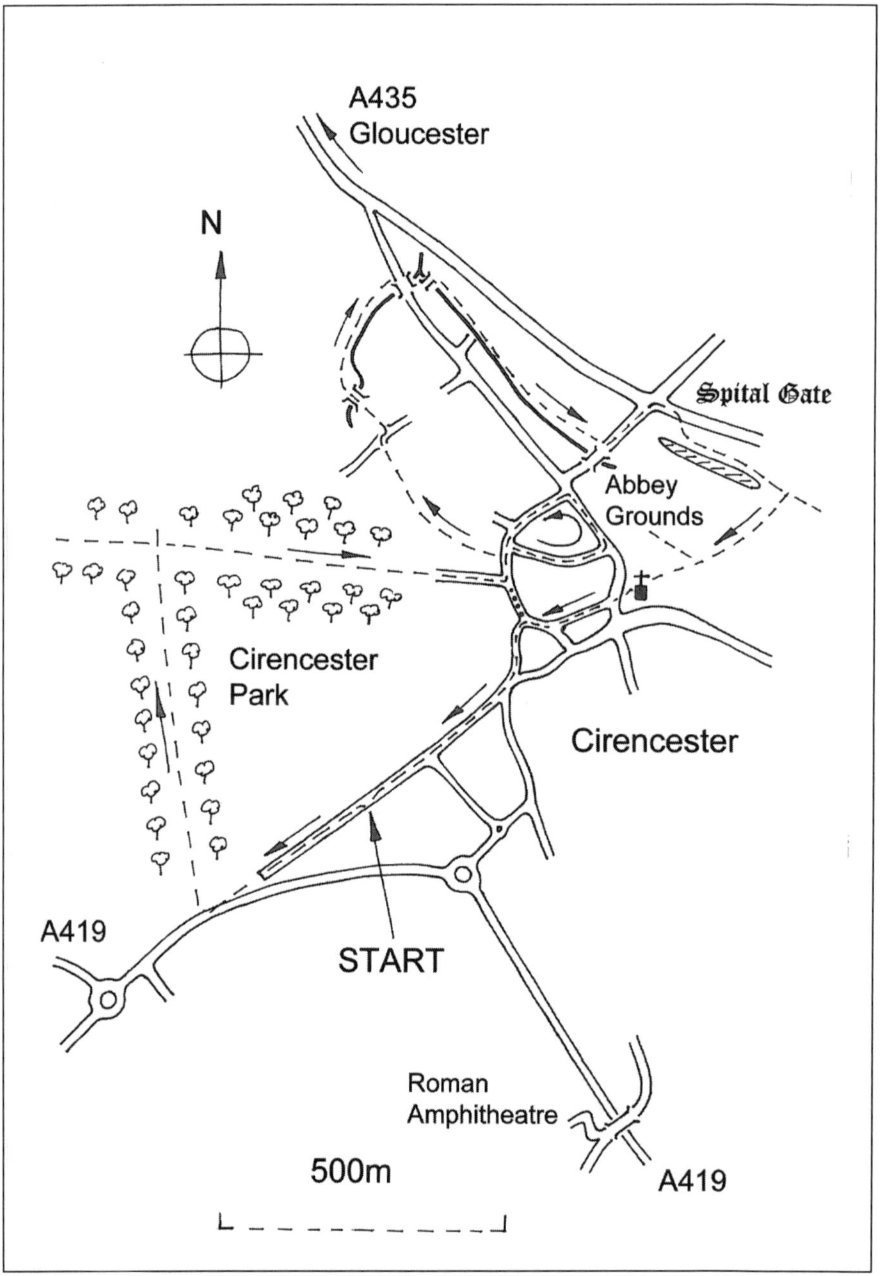
A435
Gloucester
N
Spital Gate
Abbey
Grounds
Cirencester
Park
Cirencester
A419
START
Roman
Amphitheatre
500m
A419

✓*This old post box has the letters GR on it. This stands for George Rex, which means that it was made when King George was on the throne. Older post boxes might have VR on them which means they were made when Victoria was Queen.*

Q3 Most post boxes now have ER on them. What do you think the E stands for?

You have now returned to the top of Coxwell Street. Walk on for a few metres and turn right onto a path sign-posted 'Riverside Walk'. Follow this to a road (Barton Lane) where you turn right and then immediately left onto a path between a wall and a hedge. After crossing a bridge this becomes a delightful river-side path shaded by **ash**, **sycamore** and **lime**.

✓There are many types of water bird along the river. Look out for moorhens (small and black with a yellow tipped red bill), coots (like the moorhen but with a white bill) and of course the ducks. The male duck is more brightly coloured than the female but the male and female moorhen are very similar to each other. As the older moorhen chicks approach adulthood they will feed the younger chicks of their parents. Not many other birds do this.

The path eventually finishes at a road where you turn right and then immediately left, passing through a narrow gap between the bridge and a wall. Cross the bridge beyond and follow the parkland round to the right, ignoring a path up to the road. Continue along the right hand side of the park and after crossing a bollarded road, press on to the end of the parkland where you turn left at a road. Walk up to the traffic lights and turn right. After 150m turn right again and walk through the 12th century Norman arch, which is the only surviving building of St Mary's Abbey. Beyond the arch turn left, and walk past a play area to reach a lake.

✓See if you can spot any swans near the lake. You are most likely to see a mute swan which has a black stripe between the eyes and an orange bill. The female is called a pen and the male, a cob. The discarded flight feathers of the pen were dipped in ink and used to write with. They were called "quill pens" but eventually the word 'quill' was left out and only the word 'pen' was used. Our present day ball point gets its name from the female swan!

Q4 What is a baby swan called?

At the end of the lake turn right and follow the path through the trees. Beyond these, ignore an inviting bridge to the left and continue straight on into the corner of the park, where the old abbey is outlined in paving stones. Bear left after the public conveniences to reach the imposing church of St John the Baptist.

Q5 What kind of bird can you see on top of the church tower?

From here continue across the road into Black Jack Street, but if time allows turn left and explore the church and the market place. The south porch of the church was built around 1500 as a business office for the Abbey. The tower is open at certain times of the year and offers a wonderful view down Broad Ride in Cirencester Park. On the other side of the market is the splendid Corn Hall which was built as a covered market in 1863.

As you walk along Black Jack Street, look out for the tiled frontage of the Butchers shop.

Q6 At one time the shop sold pickled ......?

Bear right into Park Street and pause outside the Corinium Museum.

Q7 Corinium is the Roman name for which town?

Turn left in front of the worlds' tallest yew hedge and the old gateway into Cirencester Park. * Look left at the attractive row of cottages along Park Lane and note the bricked-up windows.

✔A long time ago the more windows you had, the more tax you had to pay. To save money some people bricked up their windows. Window tax ended in 1851 so any house with bricked-up windows was built before this date.

Q8 How many bricked up windows can you see?

Follow the wall past an extended road junction, and after passing under some overhanging Yew trees you reach the Leisure Centre and the start of the walk.

Cirencester Checklist

- [ ] Stone ball
- [ ] Duck
- [ ] Horse
- [ ] Swan
- [ ] Wheely bin
- [ ] Someone walking a dog
- [ ] Horse shoe
- [ ] Clock

Walk 6. Chipping Campden

Chipping Campden was touched by a medieval magic wand and still remains spellbound. This walk takes you past many of the beautiful buildings of this famous old 'wool town' which is steeped in the history of the Cotswolds.

Distance	6km (3.75 miles)
Starting point	Chipping Campden is 4 miles east of Broadway. There is adequate roadside parking near the church on Station Road (B4035 signposted Ebrington). Alternatively, there is a car-park nearby in Cider Mill Lane. Grid Reference: 155396 Postcode: GL55 6HZ
Short cut	The walk to Broad Campden can be omitted – see text
Terrain	A straightforward walk along pavements, country lanes and well used field paths
Public toilets	These can be found in Sheep Street, which is just off Campden High Street
Refreshments	The Volunteer Inn, and various tea shops in the town. There's also the Bakers Arms at Broad Campden
Pushchairs	The route is suitable for pushchairs provided the weather has been dry for a few days. There are three kissing gates on the final section of the walk and a couple more on the Broad Campden leg which have to be repeated on the way back
Leaf collection	Alder, hornbeam, red maple and black poplar
Map	OS Explorer Map OL45

Chipping Campden

On a wet day, you can walk the puddled pavements past weathered, almost grey stonework, and easily transport yourself back to the difficult times of the early 19th century, when Campden suffered because of the decline of the local economy. On a sunny day however, the luminous stonework gleams like gold and you are reminded that when Campden was prosperous, it was a very prosperous place indeed. A sunny Campden is an unexpectedly beautiful place.

Many of Campden's finest buildings are a product of the wool trade and its wealthy merchants. Most prominent among these was William Grevel, who was a merchant at a time when wool was the major English export to Europe. In the 14th and 15th centuries Campden became the most important trade centre for wool in the area, attracting traders from as far away as Holland and Italy.

After the wool trade declined, Campden avoided the depopulation and poverty of other towns nearby thanks to one man: Sir Baptist Hicks. He was a fabulously wealthy London cloth merchant whose family had historic links with Gloucestershire. He acquired Campden Manor in 1610 and spent lavishly in the town.

Another who brought prosperity to Campden was Charles Ashbee, a follower of William Morris and Ruskin, who moved the influential Guild of Handicrafts out from London's Whitechapel in Edwardian times. Ashbee made his home in the Woolstaplers Hall and as a legacy of this artistic migration, craft workshops can still be found in The Old Silk Mill in Sheep Street.

The Walk

Turn into Church Street and soon you reach the entrance to the churchyard on the left.

✓The lime trees along the path to the church were planted in the 17th Century so they are at least 300 years old.

Q1 How many are there?

The magnificent Parish Church of St. James is a monument to the prosperity of Campden. It was rebuilt in the 15th century by the town's wool merchants, most prominently Grevel, and was further embellished by the merchants who followed him. If the church is open, wander in to the Earl of Gainsborough's memorial chapel, where you'll find an ornate monument to Penelope Noel, a young woman who died from blood poisoning after pricking herself while sewing.

Cross the road after leaving the churchyard and turn left. Pause for a moment and look back across the road to see the impressive remains of Hick's Campden House. This was once a magnificent Italianate mansion topped by astonishing spiral chimneys and a domed cupola containing a lantern as a

The Church and Pavilions Chipping Campden

beacon for travellers. It was one of the wonders of its age but was burnt down by Royalist troops who wanted to deny its use to approaching Roundheads. Only the gatehouse and pavilions remain to hint at the splendour of the great house, to which they were little more than outbuildings.

Still looking across the road, look at the old cart dip, which used to clean the wheels of carts – a sort of medieval car-wash. Walk past the almshouses and follow the road round to the right to reach the Eight Bells Inn.

Q2 How many bells can you see above the pub sign?

Turn left at the next junction into the High Street but before you do, look right for an old water pump under the shade of an **alder** tree.

✓This was one of many water pumps that once existed in the town. When this was built water wasn't supplied into your home like it is now. If you were a child in Victorian times, fetching water from this pump might have been your first job in the morning. Filling a bath would take a long time, so the whole family would use the same water to bath in! The parents bathed first, then the children and last the baby. By this time the water was filthy and you could lose the baby in it. This is where the saying 'throwing the baby out with the bath water' came from!

Q3 When was the pump made?

Return to your route down the High Street. Across the road, modest yet magnificent with its sundial and gargoyles, is William Grevel's house. Built around 1380, its gothic windows and delicately carved stonework defy you to shift your gaze elsewhere.

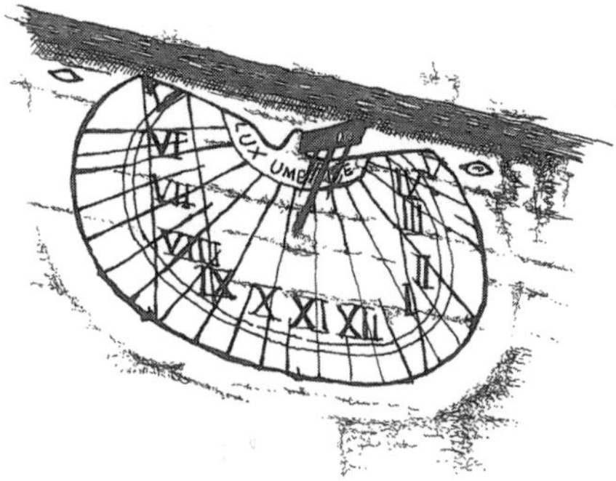

Further along, you come to the Market Hall built by Sir Baptist Hicks in 1627 for local traders. As you pass it look left for The Old Police Station, now an information centre containing a wide selection of guides, maps and souvenirs.

Q4 When was the Police Station built? (Clue: look above the door.)

Soon you arrive at the Town Hall with its clock tower. This was originally built in the 14th century as a jail, before being used as a wool exchange and courthouse. Rebuilt in the 18th century, it was fully restored in 1897 when the new entrance porch was built for Queen Victoria's Diamond Jubilee.

Q5 When was the Town Hall built? (Clue: look just above the window.)

As you pass the Town Hall, look left for the Noel Arms Hotel, which was formerly a coaching inn called 'The George'. The arched entrance once led to a stable yard and further on to George Lane, a packhorse track used to carry wool from Campden to Bristol and Southampton. In the 1790s there was a twice-weekly service to London and it was an important coaching inn throughout the 18th and 19th centuries.

Continue across the top of Sheep Street (and its public conveniences) to reach the Lower High Street. Soon you reach the relatively modern Church of St. Catharine which was built in 1891. A fine building in late Gothic style, it is worth a visit to see the stained glass windows made locally in the early 20th century.

Go straight on at The Volunteer Inn and walk along Park Road. Where this finishes, turn left and walk up through Westington. Cross the road to face

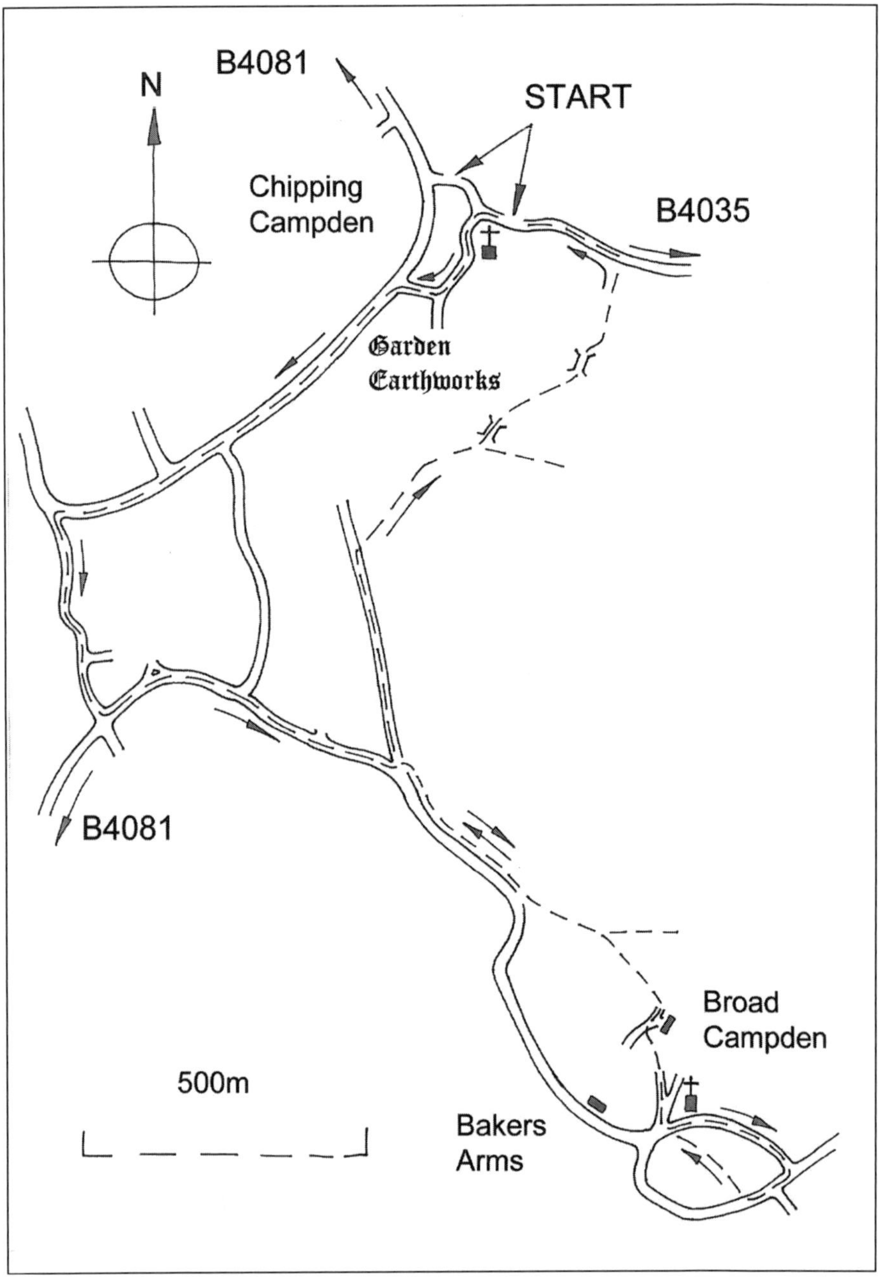
B4081
N
START
Chipping
Campden
B4035
Garden
Earthworks
B4081
Broad
Campden
500m
Bakers
Arms

on-coming traffic and take care where the road climbs round a left hand bend. After this, cross to the left of the road before it narrows near Top Farm to maintain good visibility. Continue past 'The Leasowes' to reach a road junction. Turn left here, and walk past a **hornbeam** to reach an old post box.

✓ Look at the letters VR on the post box. These letters stand for Victoria Regina which means that this post box was made when Queen Victoria was on the throne.

Q6 Most post boxes now have ER on them. What does the E stand for?

Continue past some wonderful thatched cottages.

✓ Look up at the thatched roofs. At one time all cottages had roofs made out of straw because there was nothing else available. After a while, birds would take bits of straw away to build nests and it would start to get a bit thin in places. This would become a problem in the bedroom when bugs and bird droppings would fall onto your bed. Ugh! They made a bed with a post at each corner and hung a sheet over the top to catch everything. This became known as a four-poster bed!

When the road bends left at a road junction, go straight on, sign-posted Broad Campden. Look up at the roof of a cottage near the road junction.

Q7 What kind of animals can you see on the roof top?

Eventually the road bends right near a gap in a hedgerow and a left turn to the recreation ground.

You have a choice here. To extend the walk to Broad Campden, go through the gap in the hedgerow and turn sharp right, following the course of the road from behind the hedge.

(*Alternatively, shorten the walk by turning left into St Georges' Lane, and pick up the directions again where shown* *.)

The route ahead can be seen climbing the next field on a hard well-used path. (*Pushchairs may find it easier along the nearby road, which is carefully crossed further down to reach the second field through a gap in the hedgerow*). At the top of the second field, bear right at a fork in the path to reach a kissing gate under the shade of a **red maple**.

After this, stay with the fence until you cross a tarmac drive to reach a kissing gate beyond a line of trees. Follow the path beyond into Broad Campden, passing the Quaker Meeting House, to reach a narrow lane which drops past the village green to a pretty Victorian church.

✓The bench by the church was placed here to celebrate the Queens' silver jubilee. This means that she had been queen for 25 years.

Q8 In what year was the Queens' silver jubilee?

Immediately after the church, turn left onto a lane marked 'unsuitable for motors', and follow this through the village until it climbs up to a road junction. Turn right here and immediately after 'Izod's Close', turn right again onto a narrow path. This drops down to cross a stream before climbing back to the road near the parish church. Walk past the church gate and take the left fork near the cottages to retrace your steps back to St Georges Lane and Chipping Campden.

* Walk down St Georges Lane and after passing the recreation ground, look right for a kissing gate next to a driveway. After passing through this, walk down the field beyond to reach another kissing gate under the shade of a **black poplar.** After this, walk to the right of a stone arch, once part of the ornamental garden of Hick's Campden House, and cross a metal bridge. From here, bear slightly right, aiming for a way-mark post about 200m distant. Maintain your bearing after this to cross a gated footbridge, after which the path rises up towards a cottage to the right of a line of trees.

Turn left at the road and walk back to the start of the walk.

Chipping Campden Checklist

- ☐ Bell
- ☐ Round window
- ☐ Clock face
- ☐ Stone ball
- ☐ A dog made of stone
- ☐ Nesting box
- ☐ Tennis court
- ☐ Sheep

Walk 7. Stow on the Wold

A walk which explores the historic town of Stow and the charming village of Lower Swell complete with its 'Spa'. Children will enjoy the Toy Museum in Park Street, which displays toys dating back to Victorian times. Nostalgia is guaranteed!

Distance	6km (3.75 miles)
Starting point	The Tesco store, which lies on the north side of the town alongside the A429. Parking is free. Grid Reference: 192263 Postcode: GL54 1BX
Short cut	None
Terrain	Pavements, roadside paths and field paths. One long hill
Public toilets	In Stow High Street
Refreshments	Plenty of pubs and teas shops around the Square
Pushchairs	The route is suitable for pushchairs provided it has been dry for a few days. There is an uneven section across a field and a long climb back up into Stow but a determined pushchair should get round without any problems. There are four kissing gates and two stiles
Leaf collection	Sycamore, horse chestnut, beech, oak, lime and ash
Map	OS Explorer Map OL45

Stow on the Wold

Stow-on-the-Wold stands on a hill about 800 feet above sea level. This elevated position and the effects of the elements encouraged the creation of an enclosed town square. The town's main source of wealth in former times was wool, and sheep from the surrounding areas were brought to the fairs in the Square where it is said that as many as twenty thousand were sold on a good day. The roads leading from the Square to the perimeter of the town were deliberately made narrow so that the animals could be controlled more easily.

Stow's elevated position meant that the town relied on wells for water. For centuries women and children had carried water with yoke and bucket from the well on Well Lane. Water carts plied between the well and the town where the water was sold to the townsfolk at a price of a farthing a bucket. Mains water arrived in 1937, but there were still some who drank only the well water saying it tasted better.

The Church of St Edward was built between the 11th and the 15th centuries. Many features of this outstanding Cotswold Church can be attributed to the town's prosperity as a centre of the wool trade.

The Walk

Exit the supermarket car park and turn left onto the main road. At the traffic lights turn right and then fork left onto the B4077. Walk along the high grassy verge on the left hand side of the road.

Further down the branches of **sycamore**, **horse chestnut** and **beech** hang over the wide grassy verge. Eventually you pass a water trough on the other side of the road.

✓Water troughs were once quite common when people travelled by horse. This would have been a steep hill for the horse to climb, especially if it was pulling a heavy wagon. The horse could stop here for a rest and a drink.

Q1 Can you see when the water trough was made?

Continue down to the entrance to Abbotswood House.

✓Look at the stone columns by the gate. Can you see what is on top of each column? It might look like a pine cone but it is really a pineapple. Why would a pineapple be used to decorate a gateway to a big house?

Just past the entrance turn left onto a footpath which passes through a gate and a stile. Follow the path down the left side of a field to reach a stile in the bottom left corner. Cross the bridge and walk up alongside a fence to a kissing gate on the right. Ignore this, and walk on for a metre or so before turning left through a kissing gate. Pass through a couple more kissing gates to reach a lofty path alongside a fence, which soon passes between a couple of **oak** trees.

When the fence turns right, go straight on across a field, aiming for a distant stone cottage. Continue past a tall **lime** tree, and look for a kissing gate in a fence which approaches from the left. Turn right onto a driveway and walk through Bowl Farm. Look out for a dovecote on the right.

✓A dovecote is a house for doves and pigeons to live in! Most were built hundreds of years ago when people would eat the young birds and their eggs. This dovecote is not very old and has probably never been used as a home for birds.

Q2 When it was built? (Clue: look above the door.)
Q3 What bird can you see on top of it?

Continue along the drive which passes a distant lake.

✓Can you see any swans on the lake? You are most likely to see a mute swan which has a black stripe between the eyes and an orange bill. They are one of the heaviest flying birds in the world and are really quite special. The young swans have brown feathers and they keep these until they have nearly grown up which makes them look as if they need a wash!

Q4 What is a baby swan called?

After passing the low stone arch of Lady's Well, you reach the gate-keepers lodge at the end of the drive. The route goes straight on here, but if time allows turn right for a loop around the village of Lower Swell. (*There is a gravel drive in the village so pushchairs may want to leave this section out. Pick up the directions again where shown *.)*

Soon you approach the Golden Ball Inn where you turn left into Rectory Barns. After walking to the left of Glebe House your progress is watched by a pair of eyes on a weathervane to your right!

Q5 What kind of bird can you see on the weathervane?

Follow the gravel drive past some garages to reach a path which leads to a road. Turn right here and walk down to the road junction where another right turn takes you towards the village green. Cross the road and pause by the bus shelter.

Q6 How old is the bench in the bus shelter?

Walk round the green and return to the main road where you turn left. After passing the Golden Ball you eventually follow the road round a right hand bend near the gate-keepers house you left earlier.

* Follow the road until you reach Spa Cottage on the left.

On this spot, a spring belonging to an 18th century cottage was discovered to be rich in mineral deposits and in 1804 this elaborate spa was constructed. It didn't bring any prosperity to Stow, and by 1926 the well was nearly dry and the spa house had been converted into cottages.

The use of a pineapple as a decoration above the door was no accident. The Pineapple was elitist, exclusive, aspirational and fashionable, and if the spa was to attract the right sort of clientele then the pineapple was the obvious decoration. Why?

✓This building is a spa, a place where spring water was drunk. Long ago it was thought that the spring water here had healing properties, and the rich and famous would travel many miles to try it. Spas were fashionable places and a pineapple was the ideal decoration. At this time, pineapples were incredibly expensive, and most people had never even seen one except in a book. They would not survive the long journey on a sailing ship from the Caribbean, so they were grown in this country in heated greenhouses. They were very expensive because it took 2 or 3 years for the plant to produce a pineapple. Later on faster steam ships could transport them back fresh enough to eat.

Spa Cottage

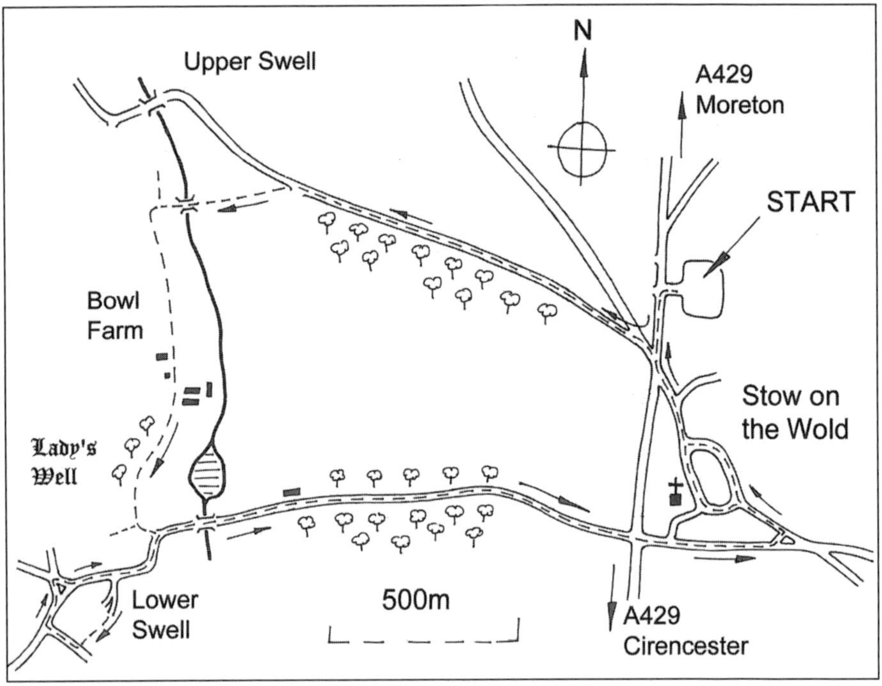

Cross the road after the cottage and follow the tree lined path up the hill. Beyond the second gate, pause by the memorial which marks the opening of the path.

Q7 When was this path opened?

Follow the path up the hill under the shade of **sycamore**, **ash** and **beech.** After the path switches sides, there are a number of tree trunks on the side of the road.

✓Look at the top of the stump and see how many rings you can count. Trees have a growth spurt in the warmth of the summer and this can be seen as a ring. Count the rings and you can tell how old the tree was.

Eventually you reach a road junction where you go straight on into Stow. Follow the road until it reaches the grassy triangle by the Royalist Hotel. The toy museum is a few metres further on, but our route takes a sharp left turn here into Digbeth Street.

Q8 Can you see when this hotel was built? (Clue: look at the sign.)

Walk along Digbeth Street to The Square. The building in the middle with the spire is Saint Edwards House.

Q9 What kind of bird can you see on the spire?

Once you've explored the square and the church, head towards the stocks which can be found under the trees on the far side.

✓A long time ago these were used to punish criminals. Their legs or arms would be fitted through the holes and locked in place. They might be left here for days. Is this worse than the 'naughty step'?

From the stocks walk round to the right and exit The Square along High Street and its public conveniences.

Further along the High Street, pause by the two post boxes on the left.

✓ Most post boxes have the letters ER on them. This stands for Elizabeth Regina which means that the post box was made when Queen Elizabeth the Second was on the throne. This is normally written as ER II, where an 'I' represents the number one in Roman numbers. The two ones are added together to make two. Can you see the second post box isn't quite the same?

It has VII on it. The V is the number 5 in Roman numbers. The 'E' on this one stands for Edward the Seventh who was King between 1901 and 1910.

Follow the High Street out to the A429 where a right turn takes you back to the supermarket and the start of the walk.

Stow on the Wold Checklist

☐ Stone ball	☐ Red telephone box
☐ Sheep	☐ Round window
☐ Swan	☐ Clock
☐ Wheely bin	☐ Post box
☐ Bell	

Walk 8. Tetbury

A walk along a leafy track to reach Tetbury, a medieval market town famous for its woolsack race and Royal connections. The route takes you along many of its famous old streets and antique shops before reaching the Chipping Steps, probably the most photographed part of the town.

Distance	6km (3.75 miles)
Starting point	About 2km north-east of Tetbury on the A433 Cirencester Road, a minor road heads south to Long Newnton. After about 750m look out for a post box just before a left turn to Ashley and Culkerton. Park on the roadside verge opposite the post box. Grid Reference: 909942 Postcode: GL8 8RU
Short cut	None
Terrain	An undulating walk over tracks, grassy footpaths and busy pavements
Public toilets	At the end of Chipping Street
Refreshments	Many tea shops and pubs in the town centre
Pushchairs	The route is suitable for pushchairs provided the weather has been dry for a few days. There is one kissing gate but no stiles. Some perseverance is needed over a 200m section of path beyond Little Larkhill Cottage, but the rest of the route is straightforward
Leaf collection	Oak, ash, alder and lime
Map	OS Explorer Map 168

Tetbury

Tetbury is justly proud of its royal connections and historic town centre, but the big attraction here is the woolsack race held every Whitsun bank holiday. This takes place on Gumstool Hill where teams of runners compete with 65lb bags of wool on their backs. It's part of a tradition dating back to the 17th century when young drovers attempted to impress the local women with feats of endurance and strength. There's plenty of other entertainment before the late afternoon finale, when the best competitors attempt to set new records in this historic event.

Tetbury thrived as a wool town in the Middle Ages and became home to one of the country's best known wool and yarn markets by the 16th century. The town centre is dominated by the splendid pillared Market House, which was built in 1665. When the wool trade declined in the early 19th century, brewing took its place as the most important local industry. The jewel in Tetburys' crown is undoubtedly the Parish Church of St Mary, which has one of the highest church spires in the country.

More recently the town has benefitted from Royal patronage. Highgrove, home of HRH the Prince of Wales is situated just outside Tetbury, and Gatcombe Park, home of the Princess Royal is also nearby. There is even a fruit and vegetable shop in the town selling produce from the Highgrove estate, and many shops in the town bear the three feathers of the royal warrant.

The Walk

Opposite the turning to Ashley and Culkerton, turn into a lane signposted 'Little Larkhill Cottage'. Soon the distant spire of Tetbury Parish Church appears on the horizon as you pass to the left of some pine trees.

✓Pine trees are 'evergreens' which means they keep their leaves all year round. They carry their seeds in cones. See if you can see any on the ground. They are grown for their wood which is used to make furniture.

Continue along the track which soon crosses a cattle grid before eventually arriving at Little Larkhill Cottage.

Q1 What animals guard the gate?

Bear left at the gate and follow a grassy path which passes to the left of the cottage. This becomes a little uneven for about 200m near a power line, but will not deter a determined pushchair!

✓In spring you may hear something tapping on wood. This will be a woodpecker. It uses its beak to make a hole in a tree trunk to nest in. They have two toes pointing forward and two backwards to help them cling to the trunk of the tree. They have a long and sticky tongue, which helps them find insects under the bark.

Soon you pass through a gate before dropping down to a track. Ignore the gate on your right, but note the gate ahead of you which leads to Herd Lane. This is your route back, but for now turn left onto a broad tree-lined path.

✓You are now walking along the path of an old railway line, which closed about 50 years ago. All the trees along the track have grown up since the line closed, so they will all be less than 50 years old. They are trying to grow as quickly as possible, and the **ash** and **alder** trees seem to be winning the race. Look out for an **oak** tree. If you see one, look how small it is compared with the other trees. Oak trees grow slowly but can live for over 500 years. In 200 years time, the ash and alder will have died, but the oak will still be quite a young tree.

Q2 What are the seeds of the oak tree called?

Eventually you reach the end of the line, where you fork left round a car park to reach a blue-bricked goods shed; all that remains of Tetbury Station. Head for the car park exit but before you reach it, turn left and pass to the right of the shed and its period GWR benches.

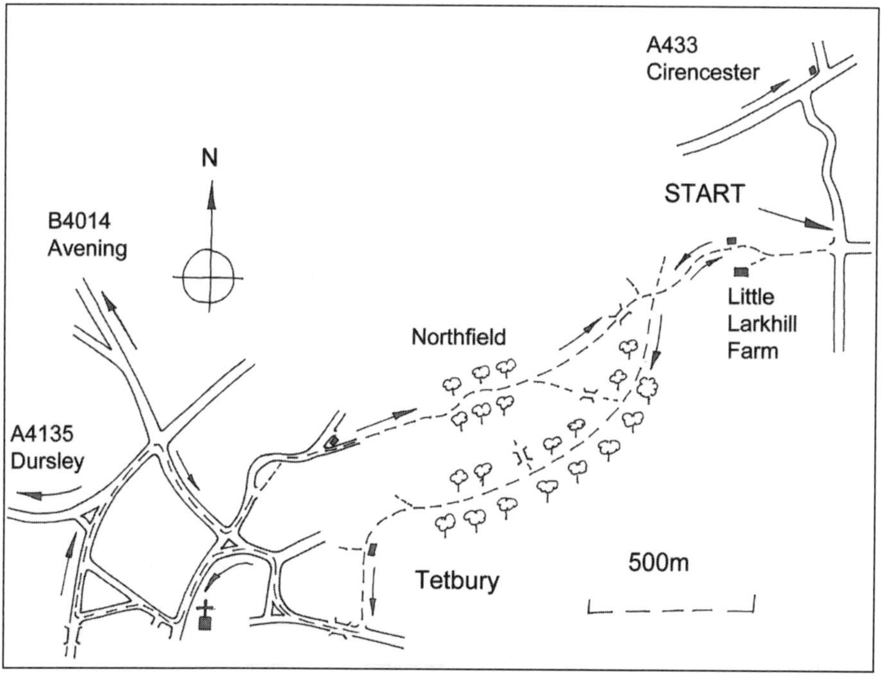

✓These benches are all that is left of the railway station which closed in 1964.

Q3 How many can you see?

Keep straight on here towards Wiltshire Bridge, ignoring the path on the right to Gumstool Hill. Continue through the landscaped railway yard to reach the road where you turn right to cross the bridge. As you begin your climb up Silver Street, pause by the telegraph pole, where a gas lamp bracket and memorial plate can be found.

✓Until 1924, when electricity became available in Tetbury, the streets were lit by gas lamps. Someone had to go round and light them all before it got dark. This person was called a lamp-lighter. In 1865 he was paid 18 shillings a week (90p in today's money). What could you buy for 90p now?

Q4 When was Tetbury first lit by gas?

Stay with the road as it climbs right and then left, crossing the top of Gumstool Hill to head towards the Market Hall. Gumstool Hill is the site of the famous woolsack race. Cross the road to reach the Post Office and pass to the left of the Market Hall.

Q5 Look at the weather vane on top of the Market Hall and the brackets on the wall. What animal can you see?

Beyond the Market Hall turn left into Church Street. Look across the road into the window of the 'House of Cheese' shop.

✓Can you see a symbol with three feathers? This means that Prince Charles buys his cheese from here, and the three feather symbol is his emblem - a sort of badge. This is quite an honour for the shop keeper and will be good for business because his customers can tell their friends that they shop at the same place as royalty. If you go into the shop, don't push in front of the Prince, and don't ask the shopkeeper to tell you what the Prince has purchased - he's not allowed to tell you!

Q6 What is the name of Prince Charles' wife?

Walk down towards the church, which was rebuilt in the 18th century in the Gothic style and is well worth exploring. Just beyond the church, turn right into West Street, and after passing the top of Black Horse Hill, fork left into Cottons Lane and walk down to Cutwell Bridge and its adjacent ford. The walk continues by turning right here, but turn left for a moment to see this former packhorse bridge which dates back to 1622.

✓Can you see what looks like a white rule sticking out of the ground near the bridge? This is a depth gauge, and if it has been raining heavily there could be quite a lot of water flowing across the road. This gauge will then be sticking out of the water so that motorists can tell if it's shallow enough to drive across.

Q7 What is the maximum depth on the gauge?

Return to your route and walk up Cutwell until it reaches a junction with New Church Street where you go straight on past the triangular green. Soon you reach the Fire Station which is shaded by **lime** trees. Pause here, and look across the road for St Saviours Church, which was built in 1848 for those who could not afford to rent a pew at mighty St Mary's. It was declared redundant in 1973 and is now under the care of The Churches Conservation Trust. It still retains much of the gas installation used to heat the church including a row of gas jets on top of the chancel screen.

Q8 What can you see standing on top of the spire?

Soon you reach a busy road junction where you turn right into Long Street. Before turning the corner, cross the road at the island and head for the old Magistrates Court which is now a Police Museum. At the time of writing admission was free.

Q9 When was the Magistrates Court built? (Clue: look above the doorway.)

Proceed along Long Street and its antique shops. Soon the Market Hall comes into view again and if you look across the street, you will see the Highgrove shop, which sells produce from Prince Charles' estate.

At the junction in front of the Market Hall turn left into Chipping Street, where the public toilets can be found about 200m down on the right near a car park. On reaching this you have a decision to make. You should really bear right across the car park to walk down the Chipping Steps. Those with pushchairs may prefer to bear left, crossing the road at the end of the car park to find a raised pavement on the other side. The road is then followed downhill until it becomes Cirencester Road (those using the steps will turn

The Chipping Steps Tetbury

right onto this) which soon bends left to reach the Royal Oak Inn. Fork right immediately in front of the pub into Herd Lane, and follow this beyond the allotments where the track bends left at a sub-station.

After passing through the trees you reach a five bar gate at the entrance to Preston Park.

Q10 What are you not allowed to do here overnight? (Clue: look at gate.)

After passing through the gate, stay with the high level path which reaches a distant pair of benches. Walk between these and pass to the right of a covert before dropping down to cross a stone footbridge near Wor Well, source of the River Avon. Follow the path beyond to a gate on the right, which allows access to the old railway line you walked earlier. Take the path opposite which climbs up to another gate and re-trace your route back to the start.

Tetbury Checklist

☐ A man walking a dog	☐ Sheep
☐ Picnic bench	☐ Round window
☐ Wheely bin	☐ Clock
☐ Red telephone box	☐ Bell
☐ Satellite dish	☐ Garden shed

Walk 9. Fairford

A walk which follows the tranquil River Coln as it meanders through the historic old wool town of Fairford. Later, the route follows leafy paths and riverbanks to reach the Cotswold Water Park. There are plenty of birds to feed, and a number of places where tired little feet can paddle in the sparkling River Coln. Come prepared, and remember to save some bird feed for the end of the walk!

Distance	**6km (3.75 miles)**
Starting point	**Drive into the centre of Fairford along the A417 and turn north into the High Street. After passing the church, turn left into Mill Lane, where a free car park can be seen immediately on the right. Grid Reference: 152013 Postcode: GL7 4AD**
Short cut	**Yes, see text and dotted route on map**
Terrain	**Flat walk along pavements, lakes and river banks**
Public toilets	**In the High Street**
Refreshments	**There are a number of pubs in the town**
Pushchairs	**The route is suitable for pushchairs provided the weather has been dry for a few days. There are three kissing gates and two stone stiles**
Leaf collection	**Willow, field maple, black poplar, sycamore and horse chestnut**
Map	**OS Explorer Map OL45**

Fairford

Fairford originated as a crossing point on the River Coln. The main street of the town is lined with 17th and 18th century stone houses and these, along with its many inns, are a reminder of Fairford's importance as a coaching centre. The town is dominated by the beautifully proportioned late perpendicular 'wool' church of St Mary with its pinnacled tower and magnificent medieval stained glass windows. They flood the church with light and were designed to tell the Bible story to a largely illiterate congregation. The stained glass has been removed several times down the centuries to save it from the hazards of war, and in 1912 they even stationed an extra policeman at the church to protect them from attack by Suffragettes! The church was completely rebuilt between 1485 and 1500 by wool merchant John Tame, who died before it was finished.

Fairford's other attraction is the huge air tattoo, held at the nearby airbase where Concorde made its maiden flight. Despite the noise, the pretty River Coln still meanders across the water meadows like it always has done, and nothing seems to disturb the heron, swans and waterfowl which can be seen along its banks.

The walk

From the car park, head towards the High Street, and after passing the war memorial, turn into the churchyard and walk up to the porch. On the left is a memorial to 'Tiddles' the cat.

Q1 Look at the top of the memorial. Can you see how old Tiddles was when he died? (You may need to use your finger to follow the numbers cut into the stone.)

Return to the High Street and turn right. Pause outside the old school.

Q2 The task of restoring the old school began in 2000. When was it finished? (Clue: look to the left of the door.)

Continue down the High Street past the Bull Hotel and the Post Office to reach a road junction. Go straight on into Back Lane and then turn right into Gas Lane. Pause by Retort House, which was the site of the local gas company.

✓The gas we use in our homes comes from the North Sea and some reaches us from as far away as Russia. Before this, most towns made their own gas at a gas works, a kind of factory where gas was made from coal. This was where gas was made in Fairford.

Q3 When did they stop making gas here? (Clue: look at the plaque on the wall.)

Soon the road becomes a path which reaches the River Coln near a **willow** Tree. Ignore the footbridge on the right, and stay on the left bank of the river.

✓There are many birds which live near the river. Ducks, swans, white geese, canada geese (black necks), moorhens (small and black with a red stripe on their heads), and coots, (small and black with a white stripe on their heads). See how many you can spot. If you see a flock of geese in flight you will notice that they fly in a 'V' formation. After the first bird has flapped its wings and pushed some air downwards, the air rises back up again and helps keep the next bird up in the air. They save a lot of energy flying this way.

Ducks and geese 'moult' in summer, which means that some of their feathers fall out to help them keep cool. They grow back again as the weather gets colder. Look out for their feathers in the grass. Cats and dogs moult. If you stroke a dog in the summer, you may notice your hand gets covered in loose hairs.

Look out for the great willowherb, which loves the damp ground near the riverbank. It is about a metre tall and has dark pink flowers with cream centres.

After following the riverside path for about 1km, look for a footbridge on the left which takes you away from the river. Immediately after crossing the bridge you have a choice. To do the full walk turn right.

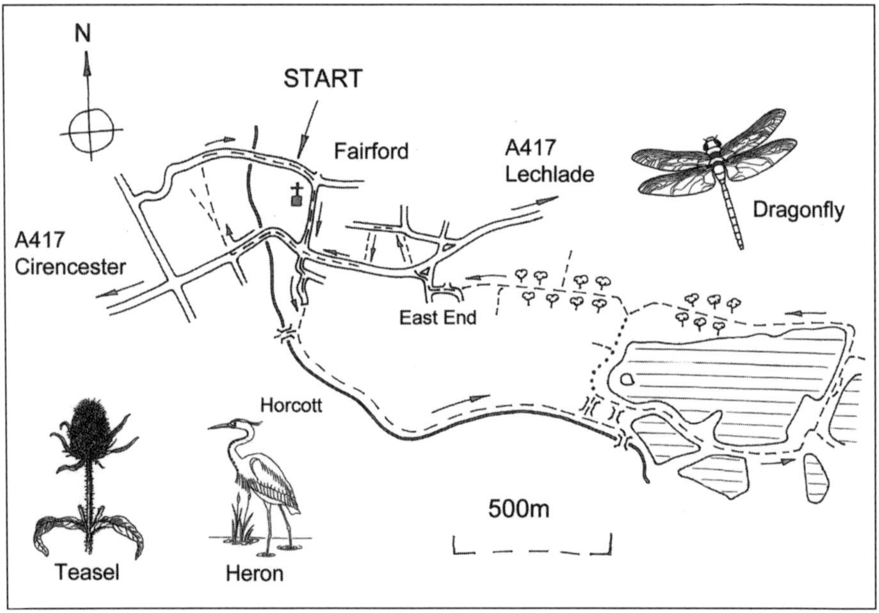

(To take the short cut turn left, and follow this path to a T-junction where you turn right. Continue to a fork where you bear left to arrive at a metal gate. Pick up the directions again where shown *.)

Ignore another bridge which soon appears on the right, and stay with the path which loops round a lake with two distinct corners. This was once a gravel pit but is now a haven for birds and flowers.

✓Keep an eye open for teasels (see map) which grow near the path. They are quite prickly and were once used in the cloth making process. They were rubbed against the cloth to make it soft and fluffy (don't try it on your own clothes!).

You may also see a thistle which is a prickly plant with purple flowers. The thistle is the emblem of Scotland. This is because an invading army from Norway tried to creep up on the Scottish Army at night. They even removed their boots so that they would make less noise. One of the invaders cried out when he stepped on a thistle. This woke up the Scots who then won the battle. You can often see a thistle on the back of a pound coin.

Q4 What is on the front of a pound coin?

After about 500m the path turns sharp left near a **field maple**, and after jogging right and left near a metal gate, it approaches the open water.

✓ The flower that looks like an oversized daisy is the ox-eye daisy, which has spoon shaped leaves. See if you can count how many petals they have. You may spot a dragonfly near the water (see map). They are large and fly very fast. They cruise along the water's edge snapping up flies and midges until the beginning of winter, when the early frosts kill them off. They will always be found near water, because they spend the first part of their lives at the bottom of ponds and rivers.

Q5 Do dragonflies sting?

The path splits in two but soon rejoins, after which you continue straight on along a grassy path, ignoring a track which bends sharp right. Eventually the path turn left again near a farm gate and after 50m passes under the branches of a **black poplar**. Its leaves seem to have been cut out of green plastic sheet. The fenced path is now arrow straight before falling under the shade of a variety of broad-leaved trees as it passes to the left of the former site of Fairford Railway Station. After emerging into the light near a crop field, you reach a junction of paths. Here you fork right and pass some knapweeds to reach a metal gate.

✓The purple flowers of the knapweed look a bit like thistles except they are not prickly. They attract many types of butterfly which like the nectar deep in the flower head. In autumn the dead flower head is full of seeds which provide food for birds during the winter.

Q6 What is a baby butterfly called?

* Follow the leafy path, under the shade of a variety of trees including **sycamore.** Eventually you reach a wall with a memorial stone.

Q7 Who is missed by all his friends?

Go straight on through a kissing gate, ignoring another path which bends left. After crossing a small field you pass through another kissing gate to reach a housing estate. Go straight on to a road junction where you turn right to reach the Eight Bells pub. Fork left at the triangle and cross the main road to find a path behind a metal barrier. After 200m the path emerges at a road junction where you turn left, signposted 'The Library'.

Q8 What is the name of the playing field on the right?

Continue along the road until you reach the hospital. Pause in front of the hospital and look at the memorial stone to the right of the front door.

Q9 If Victoria became Queen in 1837, can you work out when this stone was laid?

✓*Look at the bell pull near the door. Before people had electric door bells, the bell was rung by a rope which passed through the wall of the house.*

Immediately after the hospital turn left onto a walled path which passes under some **horse chestnut** trees before reaching the main road. Turn right here and head into the town centre.

After passing some 'take-aways' you see the front door of a boot-maker.

✓If you look above the door you will see he also did repairs. Years ago, shoes were repaired because they were far too expensive to replace. In Victorian times you would wear the shoes that you older brother or sister had outgrown. When you had outgrown them, they would be passed on to your younger brother or sister!

Go straight on at the town centre (sign-posted Cirencester A417) and soon you arrive at a bridge.

Q10 Can you tell which river flows under the bridge? (Clue: look at plaque on bridge.)

✓This stretch of river is very popular with herons. See if you can see one standing very still at the waters edge. They wait until a fish swims close by and then catch it with their long beak (see map).

Continue out of the town until you reach a footpath opposite Waterloo Lane. Turn right onto this and follow a grassy path which runs alongside a ditch to reach the far side of a field. Turn right when you reach the road and walk past a duck pond near Fairford Mill. Wander over to the railings in front of the mill and look down to see the millstream.

The Old Mill at Fairford

✓Flour is made by crushing wheat until it becomes a powder. Years ago there was no electricity to do this, so this stream was used to drive a paddle wheel which was attached to a big round stone. This would have been used to crush the wheat. There are a couple of these stones on the other side of the mill.

Q11 When was the mill built? (Clue: look on the wall above the stream.)

Continue on towards the church and the start of the walk.

Fairford Checklist

- ☐ Stone cat
- ☐ Tennis court
- ☐ Telephone box
- ☐ Stone ball
- ☐ Person walking a dog
- ☐ Cow
- ☐ Swan
- ☐ Horse
- ☐ Fallen tree
- ☐ Duck
- ☐ Round window

Walk 10. Bourton on the Water

Water is never far away on this walk, which crosses the River Windrush on six occasions as it explores of one of the Cotswold's most popular tourist destinations.

The river is invitingly shallow in places, but the gravel pits encountered later in the walk may be deep so take care over this section. There are plenty of opportunities for a paddle, and children will love the model village, built from the same Cotswold stone as the original.

Distance	7 km (4.25 miles)
Starting point	Aim for the traffic light controlled junction north-west of the village on the A429. Turn into Station Road here and after about 400m turn left into Meadow Way where a car can be left on the road-side. Grid Reference: 168214 Postcode: GL54 2HG
Short cut	Yes, see text and dotted route on map
Terrain	Level walk along well-used grassy paths, busy pavements and country lanes
Public toilets	Facilities at the Birdland car park
Refreshments	More than enough in the centre of the village. Possibly the only place in the Cotswolds where candy floss is readily available!
Pushchairs	It would be best to take the short cut. There are four kissing gates to negotiate but provided the ground is dry underfoot, there shouldn't be any problem
Leaf collection	Lime, ash and black poplar
Map	OS Explorer Map OL45

Bourton on the Water

Bourton is the most popular tourist attraction in the Cotswolds. The centre of the village is unashamedly pretty, with ornamental stone bridges spanning the sparkling waters of the River Windrush.

The arrival of the car in the 20th century brought a considerable amount of holiday traffic to the village, and the scale of the local tourist industry increased considerably. The Model Village opened as long ago as 1937, and this has been joined by newer attractions such as Birdland and the Motor Museum. This has resulted in an increasing number of tea-shops, souvenir shops and guest houses, but despite it all, on a quiet day Bourton can still create an atmosphere of calm beauty. Many fine Cotswold stone buildings flank its broad village green, and grassy lawns lead right to the water's edge, where willows hang over the river.

Away from the crowds at Bourton

The Walk

Walk back to the junction of Meadow Way and Station Road and turn left. After 30m, turn right onto a footpath behind a metal barrier. Beyond some more barriers the path is shaded by an avenue of **lime** trees as it passes a couple of schools. Eventually, just before the churchyard, turn right at more barriers onto a narrow lane, which passes in front of a school.

Q1 When was the school built? (Clue: look up near the roof.)

As the lane drops left, go straight on along a tarmac path. This eventually crosses a lane where you continue on past some lock-up garages. Soon you reach a junction of paths near a disused railway embankment. Ignore the path over the embankment in favour of a left turn which squeezes between some cottages to reach Lansdowne Road. Take care here because this is the main route in for tourist traffic.

Look across the road to the right for a footpath which takes you past a row of **lime** trees. Ignore a path which soon appears on the left, and continue on to the river, one of Bourton's dreamy backwaters.

Q2 How many arches support the bridge?

✓There are often many types of water bird along the river. Look out for moorhen (small and black with a red bill tipped with yellow), coot (like the moorhen but with a white bill) and of course the ducks. The proper name for these is mallard, and like most birds the male is brightly coloured compared with the female. He will have a green head with a white band around his neck while she will be quite plain in colour. Unlike swans, they do not pair up for life.

Q3 What is a baby swan called?

Cross the bridge and turn left to follow the river-side path. After passing through a kissing gate the path eventually leaves the river to head for another kissing gate at the rear of some houses. Follow the path beyond to a road where you turn left to head into the village.

Q4 What is the name of the pub?

Walk to the river and turn right to follow the river-side path. Over to the left is the Motor Museum, which is housed in one of the village's former mills. Eventually you cross a bridge to continue your walk along the opposite bank. Alongside this bridge is a ford.

✓A ford is a shallow place where a river can be crossed in a car. They were very common at one time because they were cheaper to build than bridges. Many towns were named after fords. Oxford was a place where oxen (cattle) crossed the river using a ford so they named it Ox-ford. Can you think of any others?

Soon you leave the river behind and continue along the pavement to reach the Birdland car park and its public conveniences.

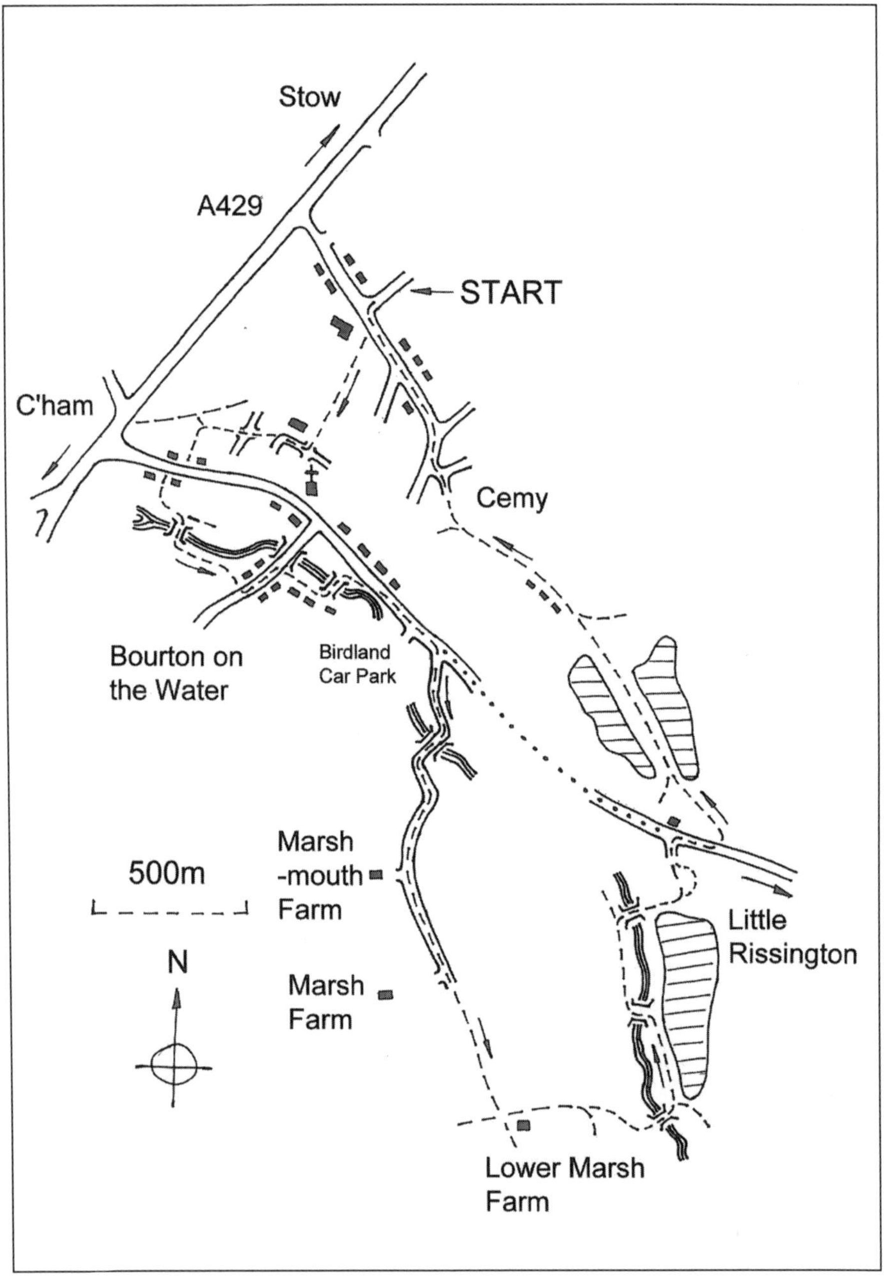
Stow
A429
START
C'ham
Cemy
Bourton on
the Water
Birdland
Car Park
Marsh
-mouth
Farm
500m
N
Marsh
Farm
Little
Rissington
Lower Marsh
Farm

*(The short cut is straight on from here. Follow the road out of the village for about 1km until you come to an electricity sub-station beyond a row of detached bungalows. Pick up the directions again where marked *.)*

About 50m beyond the car park, turn right into Marshmouth Lane, and pause in front of the first house on the left. Look at the weather vane on the roof.

✓Knowing wind direction was part of primitive mans' survival kit. It helped him to sense impending storms and make fires safely. It enabled him to stay downwind of an animal he was hunting so the animal wouldn't pick up his scent. It was also useful in battle. With the wind behind him an archer would be able to fire his arrows further than the archers in the opposing army.

Q5 What kind of animal is on top of the weather vane?

Continue down the lane until you reach Marshmouth Stables.

✓The large stone at the roadside is a 'mounting block', which is used by horse riders to get up onto their horses.

Q6 What is a baby horse called?

There is a small stable nearby. You might see a horse being ridden along the road.

✓You might see a horse make an odd expression where it curls its upper lip and bares its teeth. It looks like it is laughing but it's really trying to improve its sense of smell. It wants to know if you smell nice or not!

Q7 How many eyelids does a horse have? One, two or three?

Eventually you reach the entrance to Marsh Farm. Ignore this and go straight on along a track which soon crosses an open field to reach a house. Just before the house, turn left in front of a conifer and follow a track along the edge of the field. This eventually leaves the field behind to wander through some scrubland before bending sharp right in front of a metal farm gate. Here, look for a stile and footbridge to the left of the gate, and follow the path beyond along the edge of a small copse. Shortly, a gravelled path takes you to a substantial bridge over the Windrush. Follow the path beyond through a gate, and then turn left in front of a wooden farm gate to reach a lake.

Q8 Fill in the missing word: 'Caution, Deep _____'

✓The lakes on the right look like they have always been there but they are really flooded gravel pits. Gravel is dug out of the ground and used to make roads. When all the gravel has gone a big hole or pit is left behind. This is then filled with water to make a nature reserve. The water will be very deep here so be careful.

Look out for the Canada goose. It's a large bird with light brown feathers, a black neck and a white throat patch. It makes a honking sound. If you see a flock of geese in flight you will notice that they fly in a 'V' formation. After the first bird has flapped its wings and pushed some air downwards, the air rises back up again and helps the following bird to stay in the air. They save a lot of energy flying this way. They could achieve this by flying behind each other but they change this to a 'V' formation so they can see one another.

Q9 What is a baby goose called?

Soon the path leaves the water briefly to cross the Windrush again before tunnelling through a copse.

✓This little wood is dark and mysterious. It may be quiet but there are eyes watching you. Squirrels and rabbits are keeping still, waiting for you to pass by before they move again.

As you leave the copse, ignore the path ahead and turn right onto a wide wooden bridge. Go straight on along the gravel track until it swings to the left. On the outside of the bend, cross a stile and turn left, following a path which runs parallel to the track before rejoining it using a stile next to a farm gate.

Continue to the main road, where ahead of you a nicely built electricity sub-station can be seen on the other side. This demonstrates that even as far back as the 1950s, Bourton was sensitive to the demands of the tourist industry and the need for functional buildings to blend in with their surroundings.

Cross the road to the substation and turn right.

Q10 What year was the sub-station built?

* After leaving the sub-station behind turn left after about 30m to follow a path across a paddock.

At the far side of the paddock, look for a kissing gate shaded by a tall **black poplar**. After passing through this, turn left and then immediately right, following a track to the left of a flooded gravel pit.

Continue past a camp site and follow the now grassy path as it passes the rear gardens of some houses. After passing to the left of a five bar gate, turn left onto a gravelly lane. Soon you pass the entrance to some allotments.

✓Allotments date back to Victorian times and were small pieces of land given to poor people so that they could grow their own vegetables. In the two world wars, food was short and many more allotments were created so that people wouldn't starve. The huts are used to store tools and some of the allotment owners can be found in their huts smoking a pipe and listening to the radio.

The track becomes a metalled lane as it bends right near the gabled entrance to a cemetery.

Q11 When was the entrance gate to the cemetery built? (Clue: look up.)

Soon the lane reaches a busy road where you turn right. This is Station Road which soon begins a gradual left turn where it makes a junction with Roman Way.

Continue along Station Road until you see Meadow way on the right and the start of the walk.

Bourton on the Water Checklist

- ☐ Stone ball
- ☐ Stone mushroom
- ☐ Wheely bin
- ☐ Duck
- ☐ Clock
- ☐ Red telephone box
- ☐ Black crow
- ☐ Horse
- ☐ Lake
- ☐ Swan
- ☐ A person fishing

Walk 11. Yes, I remember Adlestrop

An undulating walk between two enchanting Cotswold villages, both clothed in the honey coloured stone so typical of the area. The quiet woodlands and sleepy villages are a delight, but the real discovery is the medieval wall painting in Oddington church.

Distance	8km (5 miles)
Starting point	About 1km west of Adlestrop, the A436 Stow on the Wold road crosses the Oxford to Wolverhampton railway. Just east of the bridge is a minor road which heads north to Adlestrop and Evenlode. Turn onto this and park on the roadside verge. Grid Reference: 237264 Postcode: GL56 0YF
Short cuts	Two, both shown as dotted lines on the map. The first involves a walk back along the A436. It has wide grassy verges and is not a busy road, but it is well aligned, and traffic will be moving quite quickly
Terrain	Undulating walk along estate tracks and minor roads
Public toilets	Only those available to the patrons of the Fox Inn and Daylesford Organic Farm Shop
Refreshments	See above
Pushchairs	The route is suitable for pushchairs provided it has been dry for a few days. Beyond Daylesford Farm Shop there is a short uneven section down the side of a field
Leaf collection	Beech, oak, horse chestnut and ash
Map	OS Explorer Map OL45

Adlestrop

Adlestrop Station was immortalised in verse by Edward Thomas, who made an unscheduled stop there just before the outbreak of World War One.

The area has another literary association. Jane Austen's uncle, Thomas Leigh, was rector at Adlestrop and lived at the Rectory (now Adlestrop House) opposite the church. Jane Austen's letters reveal that she visited the village at least three times between 1794 and 1806. After the gardens of Adlestrop Park were re-fashioned by Humphrey Repton, she used them as a setting for her novel *Mansfield Park.*

The Walk

Walk back to the A436 and turn left, following the roadside path until you reach a right turn to Kingham. Opposite this, turn left onto a track which passes to the left of a gatehouse, once part of Adlestrop House.

Q1 When was the gatehouse built? (Clue: look up towards the roof.)

Follow the gravel track through the grounds of the estate until it ends just beyond a cricket pitch. From here, walk straight on towards a five bar gate about 50m away. Beyond this, follow the path round to the right, and walk up to another gate on the outskirts of Adlestrop. Pause for a moment beyond the gate under the shade of a **beech** tree.

✓Look at the nut shells on the ground. These have fallen from the beech tree and squirrels love to eat them. In autumn there are more nuts than they can eat, so they bury some for the winter months. Sometimes they forget where they buried them and the nuts grow into a tree. Do you sometimes forget where you leave things?

Q2 You are most likely to see a grey squirrel, but what other squirrel lives in this country?

Continue on to the parish church, where the track becomes a road as it passes the entrance to the churchyard.

✓The arch over the entrance gate was built in 1897 to celebrate Victoria's sixtieth year as queen. This is called a Diamond Jubilee. Victoria died in 1901 after becoming the longest reigning monarch in British history.

Q3 Can you think of anyone else who has reigned for a long time?

Follow the road through the village until you reach a junction where you turn left to reach the post office. If it's open you might like to send someone a postcard!

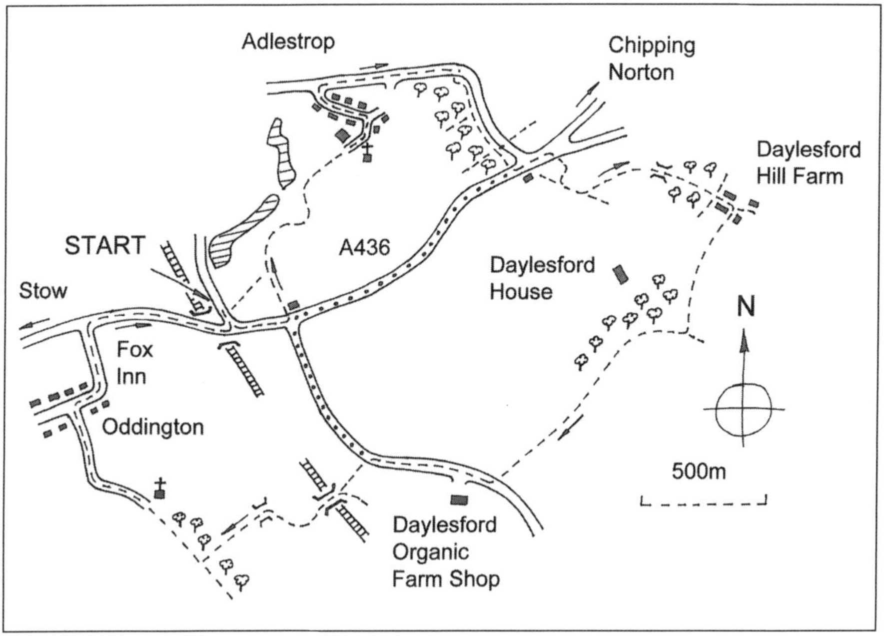

✓Look up at the roof. This is a thatched roof and you can see that it's made from a kind of grass called straw. Long ago all the roofs in the village were made from straw. Someone who builds a thatched roof is called a thatcher. Thatcher is also a common surname. At one time people didn't need surnames because they didn't travel around. If someone with the same christian name as you moved into the village, people added a surname so they wouldn't get confused. People often created a surname from the job they did to earn a living.

Q4 How many years did Dorothy Price spend working at the Post Office? (Clue: look closely at the bench.)

Walk down through the village until you reach another road junction where you turn right. Pause by the bus shelter, which lies under the shade of an **oak** tree.

✓Take an oak leaf with you – you will need it later.

The bench and name-board were rescued from the nearby station, which closed in 1966. If you look carefully, you can see Edward Thomas's famous poem on the back of the bench.

Adlestrop — only the name

Q5 How long did the blackbird sing for? (Clue: look at the words of the poem.)

Follow the lane uphill and leave the village behind. Continue past a right turn until, just before the road bends right, you turn onto a footpath on the right which leads into a copse. (*This path has a number of tree roots which make it uneven. If you have a pushchair you might prefer to stay on the road for this short section, crossing to the left side of the road to improve your visibility round the approaching right hand bend. Eventually you reach a road junction where you turn left. Pick up the directions again where shown *. Note: turning right at this road junction would enable you to escape back to the car, which is about 1200m away.*)

As you walk through the trees, ignore a path off right to a field, and later a track which crosses your path, and continue on until you reach a road where you turn left. (*A right turn at the road provides an escape route back to the car, which is about 1200m away.*)

* Walk up towards a right turn signposted Cornwell, and just before this look right for a gate which leads into some woodland.

✓Look at how dry the ground is. Trees drink a lot of water through their roots.

Q6 How much water will these trees each drink in a day? 5, 10 or 30 gallons?

Follow this path for about 150m until you reach a wooden fence. Turn right here and, keeping the fence on your left, follow it down to a tarmac drive where you turn left. Follow this track through the parkland for about 150m until two trees appear on the left. Turn left onto a farm track immediately beyond these two trees, but take a good look at them as you pass by.

✓This is the Holm oak and is unusual because it keeps its leaves all year round. Most oak trees lose their leaves in the autumn. Compare its leaves with the oak leaf you found earlier. Can you see how much tougher the Holm oak leaf is? This helps it survive the frosts of winter.

Q7 What are the seeds of the oak tree called?

Return to the route, which passes between some paddocks before crossing an ornamental stone bridge to reach some woodland. After passing an avenue of **horse chestnut** trees, you reach a junction of tracks where you go straight on into Daylesford Hill Farm.

Q8 What is the speed limit here?

As you walk through the extensive stable blocks look at the little triangular windows on the right.

Q9 How many triangular windows can you see?

Soon you reach Hill Farm Cottage where you turn right. Follow the estate road as it falls gently downhill away from the farmyard. Walk down through the paddocks until you pass a lay-by on the left. Have a look at the tree trunk in the lay-by.

✓Look at the round end of the trunk and see how many rings you can count. Trees have a growth spurt in the warmth of the summer and this can be seen as a ring. Count the rings and you can tell how old the tree was.

Continue along the road, which follows a wall round a right hand bend. After this, a small crop of lavender can be seen on the left.

✓Walk over to this and crush some of the flowers and leaves between your fingers. What can you smell? This plant was brought into this country by the Romans, and it has many uses. Moths don't like it so it was placed in wardrobes to stop them eating people's clothes. You may have some at home in a bowl to make the house smell nice.

Q10 Do you know what this plant is?

Continue for about 800m until you reach a minor road.

✓Can you still smell that plant on your fingers?

Turn right here and follow the road to round to Daylesford Organic Farm Shop, taking care to avoid on-coming traffic. Beyond this, pick up a narrow pavement and follow the road round a right hand bend. As the road straightens up briefly, look for a footpath on the left, which leaves the road to hug the right hand side of a field. (*Your second escape route is to stay with the road until it eventually reaches a T-junction where you turn left to reach the start of the walk.*)

At the end of the field, turn right onto a track which crosses a railway line.

Q11 What is the weight limit on the bridge?

Continue along the track, which passes some **ash** trees before crossing the River Evenlode using a metal bridge. After climbing gently up to a tree-lined ridge, you turn right at a T-junction to follow a track to Oddington Church and its medieval wall painting.

Walk into the churchyard and pause in the entrance porch.

✓Some parts of this church are almost 1,000 years old and date back to the Norman Conquest. Walk over to the tower and see if there are any faces looking down at you! Before you go into the church, look at the cuts that have been made in the stone seat in the entrance porch. These may have been made by soldiers sharpening their swords before going into battle. Also, the steps down into the porch are quite worn because of the number of people that have used them.

Beyond the door, the clock has stopped somewhere around the middle ages. The main wall painting on the north wall, the 'Doom' (Last judgement), was painted around 1340 and may be the largest of its kind remaining in Britain. If you look carefully, you can still see the righteous being welcomed into heaven by the angels.

The impact of this painting, now blunted by its poor condition, would have been incredibly profound on medieval worshippers at Oddington Church.

Entering through the south porch, they would have been immediately confronted with a vivid depiction of the damned going to Hell.

Continue into the village of Oddington and turn right at the T-junction. Pause by the old Post Office.

Q12 When was the old Post Office built? (Clue: look up on the wall.)

Follow the road through the village as it bends left near the local pub.

Q13 What it the name of the pub?

Follow the road out of the village until it makes a T-junction with the A436 Stow road. Turn right here using a footpath that appears just before the junction. Follow the roadside path, which switches sides just before crossing the railway. If you peer over the left hand parapet of the bridge, you can see the site of the station that inspired the famous verse and discover, like many before you, that nothing now remains.

Continue for a few metres until you reach the left turn to Adletrop and Evenlode and the start of the walk.

Adlestrop Checklist

☐ A fallen tree	☐ Telephone box
☐ Wooden bridge	☐ Railway line
☐ Horse jump	☐ Cow
☐ Horse	☐ Sheep
☐ Wheely bin	☐ Post box
☐ Horse shoe	☐ A fox (maybe not a real one!)
☐ Helicopter warning sign	

Walk 12. Bibury

Picture postcard cottages, riverside walks, a Jacobean Mansion and a trout farm! Bibury has many attractions and children will love to feed the water-birds so come prepared. If they look carefully they might even spot a trout in the sparkling River Coln. The beautifully landscaped trout farm is well worth a visit and children will love the opportunity to feed the fish.

Distance	4km (2.5 miles)
Starting point	Head into the centre of the village, where the Swan Hotel can be found next to the River Coln. Start the walk from a car park, which lies across the bridge from the hotel. Grid Reference: 115069 Postcode: GL7 5NW
Short cut	None
Terrain	An undulating walk over tracks, grassy footpaths and busy pavements
Public toilets	Near the Swan Hotel
Refreshments	There is a tea shop and a pub in Arlington
Pushchairs	Not suitable
Leaf collection	Lime, oak, ash, horse chestnut and sycamore
Map	OS Explorer Map OL45

Bibury

Turn up at the Swan Hotel on a quiet spring morning and the appeal of Bibury is immediate and obvious. In front of the hotel the water-birds splash about near the bridge, while the old mill looks down on trout swimming in the crystal clear water. What isn't so obvious is that the village was once a busy cloth making centre.

Arlington Row is a line of old weaver's cottages, and might be the most photographed Cotswold scene. After weaving, the cloth was sent to the nearby Arlington Mill for fulling before being hung out to dry. The expanse of water meadow in the centre of the village is still known as Rack Isle, after the racks that were used to dry the cloth.

The Walk

Walk over the bridge towards the Swan Hotel and see if you can spot any trout in the river. After crossing the bridge turn right.

✓There are many different water birds near the river. Ducks, swans white geese, canada geese (black necks) moorhens (small and black with a red stripe on their heads) and coots (small and black with a white stripe on their heads) see how many you can spot.

Coots are quite territorial and rather bad tempered. They will sometimes charge at other water birds for no good reason. They have lots of enemies. Their eggs are eaten by all sorts of animals such as grass snakes, crows and magpies. If you see a group of them panic and suddenly crash dive it's because a dangerous sparrow hawk may have just flown overhead.

Ducks and geese 'moult' in summer which means that some of their feathers fall out so they can keep cool in the warmer weather. Look out for their feathers on the river bank. The feathers grow back as the weather gets colder.

The Swan at Bibury

The female swan is called a pen and the male, a cob. The discarded flight feathers of the pen were used to write with. They would be dipped in ink and were called 'quill pens'. Eventually the word 'quill' was left out and only the word 'pen' remained. Our present day ball point gets its name from the female swan!

Q1 What is a baby swan called?

When the road bends left, go straight on along a road signed as 'No entry'. Soon you reach the church and the adjacent school. Look at the weathervane on the school chimney.

✓Knowing wind direction was part of primitive mans' survival kit. It enabled him to stay downwind of an animal he was hunting so the animal wouldn't pick up his scent. It was also useful in battle. With the wind behind him an archer would be able to fire his arrows further than the archers in the opposing army.

Q2 What can you see on top of the weathervane?

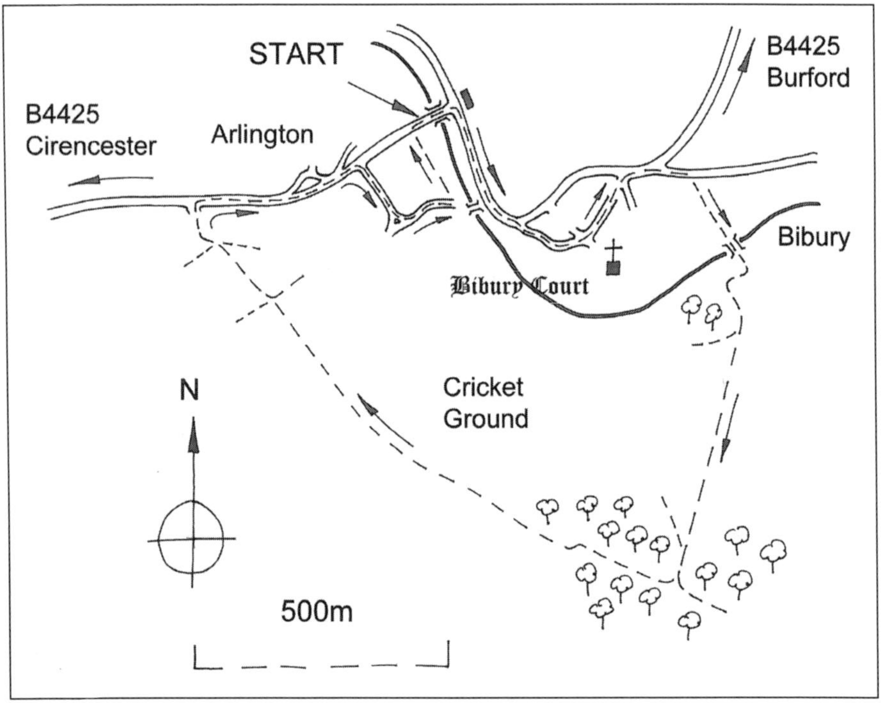

Follow the road as it bends left and stay with it as it climbs up to a small green. Beyond this, turn right at the main road, ignoring a minor road over your right shoulder.

Soon, when the main road swings left, go straight on along a road signposted Coln St, Aldwyns. After about 100m, turn right onto a private road which is also a public bridleway. This soon passes the front lawn of Bibury Court Hotel, a Jacobean Mansion dating back to 1633. Cross the bridge and walk past Bibury Mill, after which you turn right at a dovecote.

✓The pattern of holes in the wall near the roof is called a dovecote. The holes were made for pigeons and doves to make their nests in, because many years ago people would eat them and their eggs. The birds mess at the bottom of this wall would have been collected and used to help things grow in the garden, a bit like horse manure.

Q3 How many holes can you see?

Soon the road bends left and climbs up past Court Farm to reach a gate. Beyond this, ignore a path on the right and go straight on along a track, which passes an avenue of **limes.** The River Coln can be seen over to the left, meandering lazily under the trees. After passing through a farm gate, pause by a sheep pen on the right.

✓This is a sheep pen where sheep would have been sheared.

Q4 What is a baby sheep called?

Soon the path climbs up into the woodland to reach a gate. Beyond this, turn right at a junction of paths and walk under the shade of towering **oak** and **ash** trees to reach a farm gate. Beyond this, follow the path along the right hand side of the next three fields.

✓Although the fields may be full of crops, there are often lots of flowers near the edge of the field. In summer, look out for the meadow cranesbill, which grows about half a metre tall. They are easy to spot because their blue/violet flowers have five petals.

Also, see if you can spot some bright red flowers with black centres growing in the crop or at the edge of the field. These are poppies. They only live for a summer, and in the autumn, their seeds fall to the ground and wait for a chance to grow. Poppy seeds need light in order to start growing, but most get buried under leaves or soil. They sometimes have to wait for years before some disturbance brings them up into the sunlight. Here the farmer has ploughed the field and brought some poppy seeds to the surface. Some of these poppies have been waiting to grow since before you were born!

The hedgerow on the right contains a number of common shrubs such as hawthorn (red berries), bramble (blackberries), and ivy. You will also see hazel, which has long dangling catkins in the spring and nuts in the autumn. Its leaves are easy to spot: they are large, almost round, and have a point at the end. The hedgerow provides shelter for a number of small wild animals, and the berries and nuts stop the birds getting hungry during the winter. There are also some young oak trees alongside the second field.

Q5 What is the fruit of the hazel called?
Q6 What is the fruit of the oak tree called?

At the end of the third field, go straight on at a junction of paths near a small **horse chestnut**. Follow this track into the village until you reach a road where you turn right. Soon you arrive at The Catherine Wheel, a long established inn. Pause just beyond its railings to see a metal ring fixed to the wall.

✓In the days when people travelled on horseback, this ring would be used to tie a horse to, while its owner went into the pub for a drink, or to book a room for the night. The smaller building on the left was once a stable. If you lived here then, one of your jobs might have been to take the horse to the stable and make it comfortable for the night.

Q7 What is a baby horse called?

Immediately after the pub turn right onto a road that climbs up past Arlington Manor and its old barn. At the top of the hill bear left, and drop down past Hawkers Hill and its huge **sycamore**. At the bottom of the hill turn immediately left after a small cottage, but before you do, take a look at Arlington Row which attracts visitors from all over the world.

Return to the path which passes to the left of Rack Isle before reaching the start of the walk. Over to the left is the 17th century Arlington Mill which once was busy fulling cloth. Over to the right is the trout farm. If you haven't seen a trout yet, here's your chance!

Bibury Checklist

☐ A fish	☐ Red telephone box
☐ Swan	☐ Someone with a camera
☐ Horse shoe	☐ A coach
☐ Sheep	

Walk 13. Naunton

Hidden valleys, leafy riverside paths and quaint golden cottages add up to a classic Cotswold walk. Children will be fascinated by the restored dovecote, where they can watch doves and pigeons flutter out of the windows.

Distance	**5km (3 miles)**
Starting point	**Naunton lies half a mile north of the B4068 Andoversford-Stow road. Park at the east end of the village by the church. Grid Reference: 113233 Postcode: GL54 3AT**
Short cut	**The short cut can be used to reduce the walk into a tour of the village – see text**
Terrain	**Minor roads and field paths, some of which might be muddy after rain. One short but steep climb**
Public toilets	**Only available to patrons of the Black Horse**
Refreshments	**The Black Horse Inn**
Pushchairs	**Not suitable**
Leaf collection	**Beech, ash and oak**
Map	**OS Explorer Map OL45**

Naunton

Naunton is tucked away in a fold of the Cotswolds and looks like it has emerged from the landscape which surrounds it. This may be due to the fact that many of its cottages are roofed with locally quarried stone slate. This was quite a prosperous local industry until Victorian times, when railways brought cheaper Welsh slate to the Cotswolds.

For nearly 200 years, the chapel has been the focus of village life. It survived the decline of congregations that saw the closure of so many others thanks to the determination of a handful of villagers. Nowhere is this more apparent than at nearby Guiting, where Sylvia Baldwin played the chapel organ from 1954 until her death in 2010.

The old vicarage was home to Reverend Edward Litton between 1860 and 1897. He was often visited by his friend from Oxford, Charles Dodgson – better known as Lewis Carroll. Litton's daughter Alice is supposed to have inspired the heroine of *Alice in Wonderland.*

Naunton's dovecote is large, having nesting holes for over 1,000 birds. It dates back to 1600, and would have been built by a wealthy man – probably the lord of the manor of Naunton. The meat of young doves was a dish for the rich, but the birds' appetite for seed made them a constant nuisance on the corn fields. From the end of the 18th century, the price of corn rose, and dovecotes became less popular, many being converted or demolished. This dovecote survived because its prime location by the river allowed it to be converted, with some irony, into a corn mill. It continued in this guise until 1952, when the reduction of the river flow made it uneconomical. It was then used to store animals and equipment until it was restored in 2001.

The dovecote at Naunton

The Walk

Walk into the churchyard and make your way to the tower, where two sundials can be seen.

✓Long ago, clocks were very expensive, and people used a sun dial instead. The angled metal arm casts a shadow across the face of the sun-dial allowing you to tell the time. At midday the sun is directly overhead, and your shadow is very short. If the sun is out, mark the length of your shadow on the ground with a couple of twigs or flowers. You will be coming back this way later and you will be able to see if your shadow has got longer or shorter.

Q1 Can you see the date on the sundial?

Walk out of the churchyard and pause by a stone bench on a grassy triangle.

✓Can you see someone's name carved into the end of the bench?

Q2 It's the name of a famous author. Who is it?

Across the road beyond a towering **beech** tree, is the magnificent old vicarage, where Lewis Carroll visited his friend Edward Litton.

Turn left and cross the bridge to reach Pixie Cottage. Turn right here and take great care as you round the blind bend. Soon some wrought iron gates lead you to the chapel and the village war memorial.

Q3 Can you see when the chapel was built? (Clue: look above the door.)

After admiring the view across the valley, exit back through the gates and turn right. Soon you pass an old water pump.

✓Water is now piped into our homes from reservoirs. If you lived in this village in Victorian times, you and your mother would walk from your home to this pump to fetch water for drinking and washing. The long handle was pulled up and down to make water come out of the spout. The water came from a spring in the ground

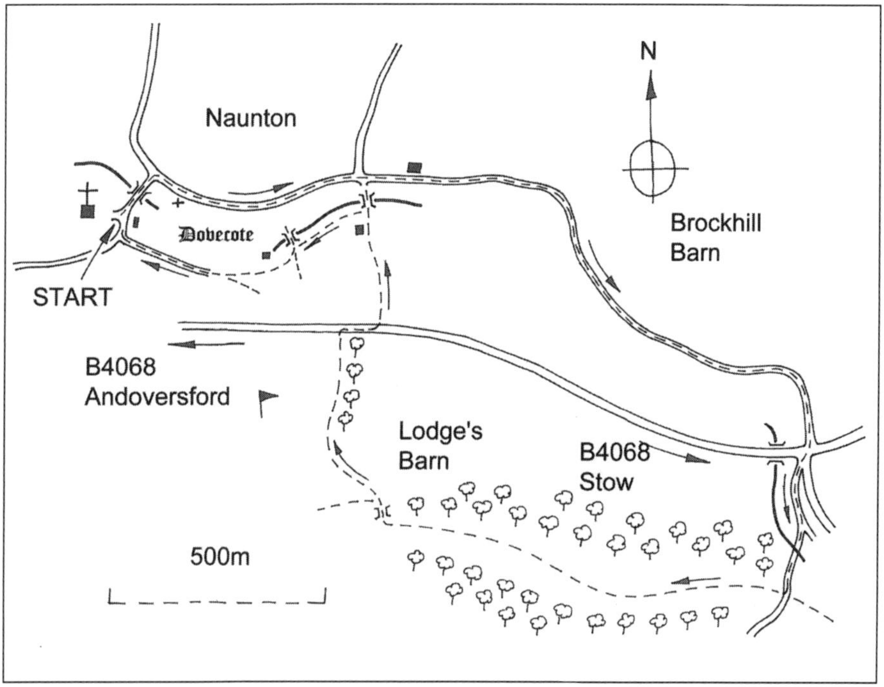

below. Some people were sad when 'tap water' arrived here 60 years ago, because they liked to meet their friends here for a chat. People didn't bath very often because it was such an effort to fetch the water. There are two more pumps between here and the village pub. See if you can spot them.

After passing the village school, continue down the hill towards the Black Horse Inn. Before you reach the pub, look left down a side road to see a weathervane.

Q4 Can you see what is standing on top of the weathervane?

Now look right to see 'The Old Band Room'.

✓The village band practised here in Victorian times.

Q5 Can you see when it was built? (Clue: look up near the roof.)

(*A right turn at the Old Band Room will shorten the walk into a tour of the* *village. Turn right after the bridge and follow the riverside path. Pick up directions again where shown *.)*

Continue past the pub and follow the road out of the village. After passing Eastern Hill Farm, an **ash** tree can be seen on the side of the road.

✓The ash is the fourth most common tree in Britain. Its wood is strong and flexible. In the past it was used by the Anglo-Saxons to make spears and shield-handles. The seeds of the ash tree hang in clusters and often don't fall to the ground until the following spring. Sometimes you can see new green seeds as well as the old grey ones from the previous year. We will see lots more ash trees later.

As you approach a right hand bend, cross to the left of the road to improve your visibility to on-coming traffic. Follow the road round to the right and continue on to a road junction. Go straight across here and take the right fork sign-posted 'Lower Harford'. Soon you see a 'Ford' sign on the side of the road.

✓A ford is a shallow place where a river may be crossed in a car. They were very common at one time because they were cheaper to build than bridges. Many places are named after fords. Hereford is one. Cinderford is another.

Q6 Can you think of a place starting with 'O' which is named after a ford?

Follow the road past the ford and continue for a short distance until you reach the 'Windrush Way' footpath on the right. Turn right onto this and walk under the trees for a short distance to a farm gate. Beyond this, follow a power line along a hidden valley.

✓Along each side of this valley are many ash trees. Some of them may still have seeds hanging in clusters from their branches.

Q7 How many seeds might a big ash tree have? 1,000 10,000 or 100,000?

Eventually you reach a stile next to a farm gate. Go straight on after this, and walk past some conifers on the right.

✓Most conifers are evergreens. This means they keep their leaves right through the winter. Conifers shed their needle-like leaves slowly during the year and new leaves grow all the time, so they are always green and never bare. Trees that lose their leaves in winter are called 'deciduous' trees. Look at the trees as you pass them. See if you can tell which are conifers and which are deciduous.

Eventually you pass through a metal gate where you turn immediately right to cross a small stone bridge. Look to the left and take the right fork which climbs steeply up a hill. As you near the top, bend right near a way-mark post and head for a gateway. Beyond this, follow a stony track alongside a wall.

✓The conifers on the right are cypress trees. Most conifers have needles but these have quite soft leaves. Look how dry the ground is under the conifers. They have been planted so close together that no light reaches the ground. It's so dark and dry that nothing grows here.

There are many young trees on your left, mainly sycamore and ash. There are no seeds on these trees because they are still too young. They will have to be between 20 and 30 years old before they have 'grown up' enough to produce seeds.

Continue straight on through the golf course and pass some young **oak** trees on the right.

✓When these oak trees are fully-grown they will take about 40 gallons of water each day from the soil. That's well over a bath-full!

Q8 What is the seed of an oak tree called?

Follow the stony track down to a road where you turn right. Take care here, although this is only a 'B' road, traffic can be moving quite quickly. After about 200m turn left onto a fenced path.

✓See if you can spot a water trough as you walk down the hill. The hillside here is quite dry so this will stop the sheep getting thirsty.

Soon the path tunnels down through a copse, and after passing the entrance to Close Hill you turn left at a bridge to follow a riverside path.

* Soon you reach the dovecote. Here you go straight on, ignoring the path sharp left. If you have time, turn right here and visit the dovecote.

✓This strange house with small windows and no door was built a long time ago for doves and pigeons to live in! People used to eat the young birds and their eggs.

Watch the birds flying out of the windows. Doves and pigeons are light grey with small round heads, little beaks and short legs. You may also see the larger woodpigeon, which is mainly grey with a white neck patch and white wing patches. They all make a 'cooing' sound.

Return to the path you left earlier and walk back towards the church.

✓Look out for another water pump along this road. As well as fetching water, the villagers in Victorian times would have used candles to light their homes. The village did not get electricity until 1948.

The same year an electric blower was installed to power the chapel organ. This relieved the need for small boys to pump it by hand! The village had to wait another 14 years for mains sewerage.

Turn right at the road junction and return to the church and the start of the walk.

✓Visit the churchyard and find the spot where you measured the length of your shadow. If the sun is still out, see if your shadow is any longer or shorter than it was before.

Q9 If you are walking in the afternoon would you expect your shadow to get longer or shorter?

Naunton Checklist

☐ Stone ball	☐ Horse
☐ Round window	☐ A person walking a dog
☐ Telephone box	☐ A person playing golf
☐ Sheep	☐ Duck
☐ Post box	

Walk 14. Miserden

A hilly but rewarding walk through the grounds of Misarden Park. The walk starts in the traditional estate village of Miserden, before dropping through the trees to find a hidden lake and a woodland stream. Although this is only a short walk, the cares and worries of the outside world are soon forgotten, to be replaced by an eerie silence broken only by your footfalls and the occasional rustle of wildlife on the woodland floor.

The walk is steep in places and directions will have to be followed carefully through the woodland areas.

Distance	5km (3 miles)
Starting point	Miserden lies 7 miles north-east of Stroud and 7 miles north-west of Cirencester, in a remote location above the secluded Frome valley. Park at the west end of the village in the school car park. Grid Reference: 934089 Postcode: GL6 7JA
Short cut	None
Terrain	Hilly walk along country roads, estate roads and well-used grassy paths which could be muddy after rain
Public toilets	None
Refreshments	The Carpenters Arms in the centre of the village
Pushchairs	Not suitable
Leaf collection	Ash, lime, horse chestnut and beech
Map	OS Explorer Map 179

Misarden Park

The valley and woods of Misarden Park are full of wildlife at all times of the year. Woodpeckers tap away at the trees in spring, herons keep watchful eye over the stream and owls hoot anonymously at dusk. There is always something to see on the lake, which is situated in an idyllic valley. In spring, the woodland floors are carpeted with bluebell, wood anemone and wild garlic, and if you are lucky, you might see a kingfisher flash across the lake.

The Walk

Walk past the village school and pause by the old school entrance between the gable ends.

✓ Look at the guttering above the door. This has been made from metal. These days it would be made from plastic and would be much lighter and cheaper.

Q1 When was the school built?

Continue past the school to the village shop and post office. There is an old water pump outside the shop.

✓Water is now piped into our homes from reservoirs. If you lived in this village in Victorian times, you and your mother would walk from your home to this pump to fetch water for drinking and washing. The pump once had a long handle which

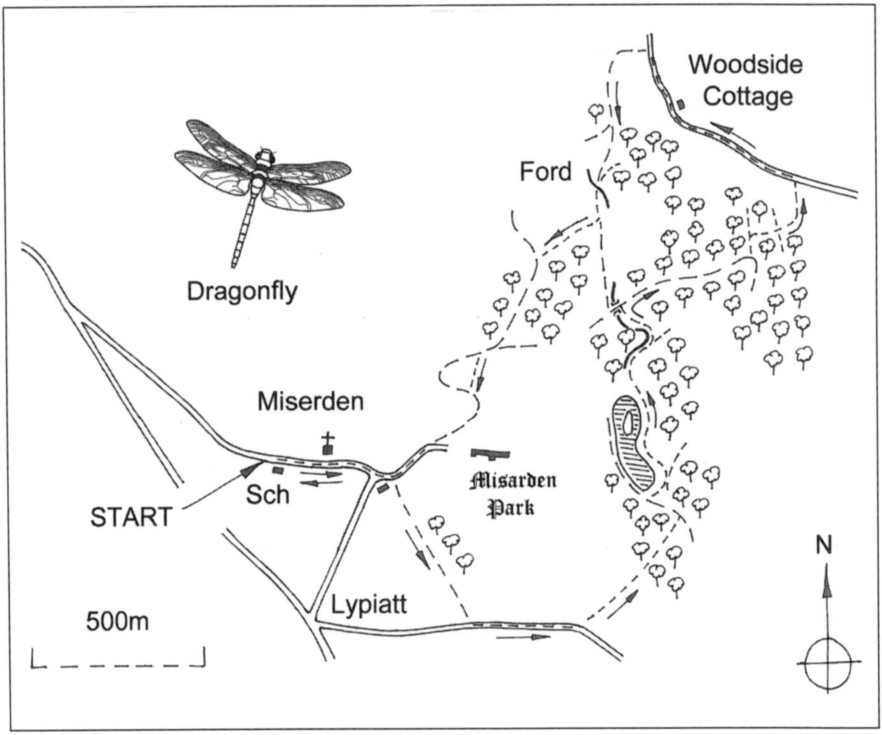

was pulled up and down to make water come out of the spout. The water comes from a spring in the ground below. Some people were sad when 'tap water' arrived here about 60 years ago because they liked to meet their friends here for a chat. People didn't bath very often because it was such an effort to fetch the water!

Continue past the village hall which has an **ash** tree in front of it. When you reach the church, walk into the churchyard and pass under a yew arch to reach the porch and its sun dial.

✓Long ago, clocks were very expensive, and people used a sun dial instead. The angled metal arm casts a shadow on the stone wall allowing you to tell the time. If it's a sunny day, find a stick and push it into the ground. Mark the end of the shadow with an object and when you come back later see if the shadow has moved. (You could do this at home. When the clock is on the hour, push a stick into the ground and place an object at the end of the shadow. Repeat this every hour to make you own sundial!)

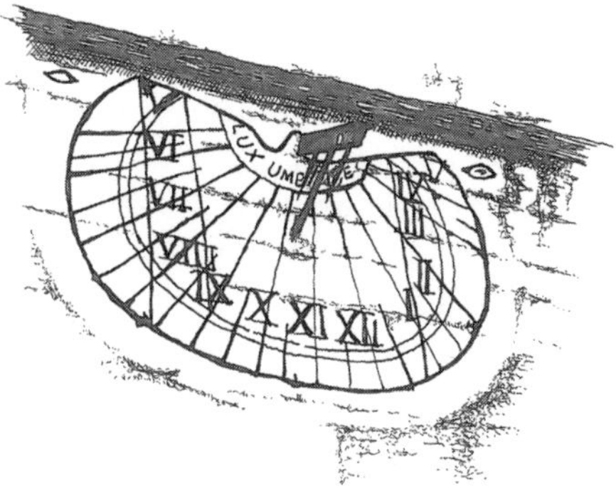

Return to the road and walk to the road junction at the centre of the village. Bear left here, and walk past the old village school, which is on your right.

Q2 Can you see when this was built? (Clue: look above the door.)

Follow the school wall round to the right to find a footpath which passes to the left of the gabled end of a cottage. Walk along the walled path under the shade of **lime** trees to reach a stone stile. Beyond this, follow a grassy path under some old **horse chestnuts** to reach a road where you turn left. After about 300m, leave the road and fork left to find a stile next to a gate. Walk down the field in front of you along a path which is marked by a slight depression in the ground. Walk down to the left of an **ash** tree.

✓The wood of the ash tree is strong and flexible and is used to make hockey sticks and handles for tools. The seeds of the ash tree hang in clusters and often don't fall to the ground until the following spring. Sometimes you can see new green seeds as well as the old grey ones from the previous year.

Q3 How many seeds might a big ash tree have? 1,000 10,000 or 100,000?

After passing through a stile at the edge of some woodland, follow a track down through the trees to reach a clearing. At the bottom of this turn left onto an estate track (be aware that the right of way cuts this corner off by walking down through the trees, but the evidence is that few people follow this route). After dropping steeply through the trees turn right at a lake and cross a footbridge. Follow the path past a wooden bench and on round the lake, ignoring another path which climbs up into the trees.

✓You may spot a dragonfly near the water (see map). They are large and fly very fast. They cruise along the water's edge snapping up flies and midges until the beginning of winter, when the early frosts kill them off. They will always be found near water, because they spend the first part of their lives at the bottom of ponds and rivers.

Q4 Do dragonflies sting?

After leaving the lake behind, the path eventually reaches a stream. As you begin to climb away from the stream, bear left at an indistinct fork to stay with the riverbank.

✓ It may be quiet but eyes are watching you. Squirrels and pheasants are keeping still, waiting for you to pass by before they move again. There are many different trees in this wood. Some are conifers and some are deciduous. Trees that lose their leaves in winter are called deciduous trees. They have large broad leaves compared with the conifers which have needles instead. Conifers shed their needle-like leaves slowly throughout the year and new leaves grow all the time so they are always green and never bare. See if you can tell which tree is which.

Conifers carry their seeds in cones. Look for some cones on your walk and take them home with you. Then leave them outside where you can easily see them. The cones open and close depending on how damp the air is. On a dry day the cone opens up and releases its tiny winged seeds which are then blown away on the wind.

Soon the grassy path reaches an estate road near a stone bridge. Turn right here and follow the road up the hill.

In the shade at Misarden Park

Eventually, when the road climbs sharply right, look for a path on the left, which is way-marked with yellow arrows as it climbs up through some young **beech** trees.

✓ If you are walking in spring look out for wild garlic. It has long smooth pointed leaves and little white flowers. If you crush the leaves between your fingers, you can smell garlic. In late spring, look for bluebells and wood anemones which have white flowers with yellow centres. In summer, look out for ferns. They have been around since the time of the dinosaurs and have hardly changed since then.

The path soon turns right and crosses an indistinct track before climbing up to a stone stile on the edge of a crop field. After crossing the stile turn left, and walk along the edge of the field to a road where you take another left turn. This road meanders down a hill (keep on the outside of the bend to improve your visibility to traffic) but before you reach the bottom, turn left onto a footpath which passes through a five bar gate.

Q5 Please close the....

Follow the track down the hill until it levels out at a junction of tracks. Go straight on here and follow the track as it bends left to reach a ford. Cross this using the bridge, and after about 150m fork right onto a path which rises up to a gate.

✓Look how dry the ground is under the conifers. When trees are planted this close together no light reaches the forest floor so no plants can grow. Trees drink a lot of water through their roots. A birch tree can absorb 30 gallons of water every day - that's almost two bath-fulls!

Q6 The seed of a horse chestnut tree is a conker. What is the seed of an oak tree called?

Beyond the gate, walk up a sunken path which soon passes to the right of a pheasant covert.

✓Listen out for the clucking call of the pheasant, which makes its nest on the ground. Pheasants are not good fliers and they spend most of their time walking around the wood looking for food. If they are frightened they will take off with a 'whirring' sound from their wings.

Shortly the path reaches an estate road where you turn left to drop down past the outstretched roots of a magnificent **beech** tree.

✓There are many tree roots on the surface of the soil here. Roots take water to the tree and also food from the soil. They usually spread over a large area which helps the tree to stay upright. Although these trees are very tall, their roots do not go very deep into the ground (usually less than 8 feet). Squirrels love to eat the nuts of the beech tree. If you are quiet you may hear them scampering along the branches of the tree.

Q7 You are most likely to see a grey squirrel. What other kind of squirrel lives in this country?

At a junction of roads at the bottom of the hill, go straight on under the branches of a **beech** tree to reach a farm gate. After this the road climbs in a big arc up the hill on your left, but unfortunately the right of way is more direct. This turns left immediately after the gate and then climbs straight up the steep incline to re-join the road just out of sight over the crest of the hill. After re-gaining the estate road follow it up into the village where you go straight on after crossing a gate and cattle grid.

Q8 The first cottage on the left was restored in what year?

Bear right at the Carpenters Arms and retrace your route back to the start of the walk.

✓Don't forget to visit the churchyard to see if your shadow has moved!

Q9 If you are walking in the afternoon would you expect your shadow to get longer or shorter?

Miserden Checklist

☐ Round window	☐ Sheep or horse
☐ Clock	☐ Stone ball
☐ Duck	☐ Telephone vox
☐ Pine cone	☐ Pheasant
☐ Greenhouse	

Walk 15. Painswick

This walk visits some of the old mills along the Painswick Brook before returning through this charming old wool town with its fine collection of Cotswold stone buildings. Leafy riverside paths take you past old sluice gates and mill ponds, which are now home to a variety of water-fowl.

Distance	5 km (3 miles)
Starting point	Look for the B4073 which leaves the north side of the town to head for Gloucester. On the edge of the town, turn east into Golf Course Road, which is signposted 'cemetery and walkers car park'. Park on the inside of the bend under the trees. Grid Reference: 868105 Postcode: GL6 6RR
Short cut	Yes – see text
Terrain	A strenuous walk along leafy paths, fields and pavements. A long ascent on the return which will test your powers of persuasion!
Public toilets	Facilities at St Mary's Street and also at the car-park south of the church
Refreshments	There are a number of pubs in the centre of the town
Pushchairs	Not suitable
Leaf collection	Lime, oak and beech
Map	OS Explorer Map 179

Painswick

Painswick is often referred to as the Queen of the Cotswolds, because of its fine collection of Cotswold Stone buildings, which were built during the heyday of the cloth making industry. The church is largely 15th and 16th century and although its churchyard is crammed with the tombs of rich wool merchants, its most memorable feature is its fine collection of yew trees. This walk passes through the churchyard and explores many of Painswick's quaint old streets.

The Walk

Walk back down the hill to the B4073 and turn left. After about 70m turn left into Gyde Road and follow it round to the right. Soon you pass the Gyde Almhouses, before Gyde House becomes visible over a wall on the left.

This former orphanage was built posthumously by Edwin Gyde, a 19th century philanthropist. While it was being converted into apartments in 2001, the workers discovered it was haunted by the sounds of children playing. It was serious enough for the builders to hire a medium to persuade the ghosts to leave. Like many new developments, security was a marketing feature and many CCTV cameras and alarms were installed. These will not provide much protection against what the surveyors' son saw on the premises: a child calmly walking through a wall.

Carry on down to the end of the road to find a gate at the bottom of a car park.

Q1 This footpath is restricted to ...... only.

Follow the path down to the A46 where you turn right. Walk along the road for about 150m until you reach Pullens Road. The last cottage on the right is Melrose Cottage, a former toll house.

✓Painswick was once quite difficult to get to, so the main road you are standing on was built in 1820 to connect Painswick with Cheltenham. The road cost a lot of money to build so people who used it had to pay a toll (a charge) to use it. The person who collected the money used to live in Melrose Cottage.

Q2 Can you work out when this cottage might have been built?

Across the road from Pullens Road is Lower Washwell Lane. Cross the road carefully and follow it as it winds down past some new houses to reach the older part of the town. Just beyond the gated entrance to Verlands, a former Victorian vicarage, turn sharp left signposted Sheepscombe, and continue down the hill. At the bottom, where the road turns sharp left, look straight ahead for a stile which leads into a field. Turn right on entering the field, and follow a wire fence to another stile.

The building on the right was once Loveday's Mill. The grass carpeted mill leat can still be seen in front of the house. The fast flowing Painswick Brook was key to the towns' prosperity but the gradual introduction of steam power to the cloth industry - and the inability of Painswick's mills to take advantage of it - led to the industries' long term decline in Painswick from about 1830.

Loveday's Mill

Cross the stile at the end of the next field, and follow the brook-side path through the trees. Beyond another stile, turn right onto a driveway, and follow it to a road. In front of you is the former Brookhouse Mill. Turn left here and then immediately right, to reach a driveway which is sign-posted 'Brookside'. Walk up to the cattle grid at the mill entrance and see the power of the mill stream.

✓This was once a mill – a kind of factory where many different things were made. At one time it made cloth out of wool and later on it made hair pins and paper clips. Electricity wasn't available at this time so this fast moving stream was used to turn a wheel which powered the machines.

This leafy track soon reaches a stable block and cottage. Walk beyond the cottage to reach a gate on the far side, after which you pass another stable to reach a five bar gate. Beyond this, walk alongside a couple of buttercup-filled meadows to reach a junction of paths.

✓If you are walking in spring or summer this field will be full of buttercups. They are slightly poisonous and horses can get an upset stomach if they eat too many of them.

Q3 What's a baby horse called?

Turn sharp right here, and walk down the track to Painswick Mill. The pond on the right was a reservoir for the mill.

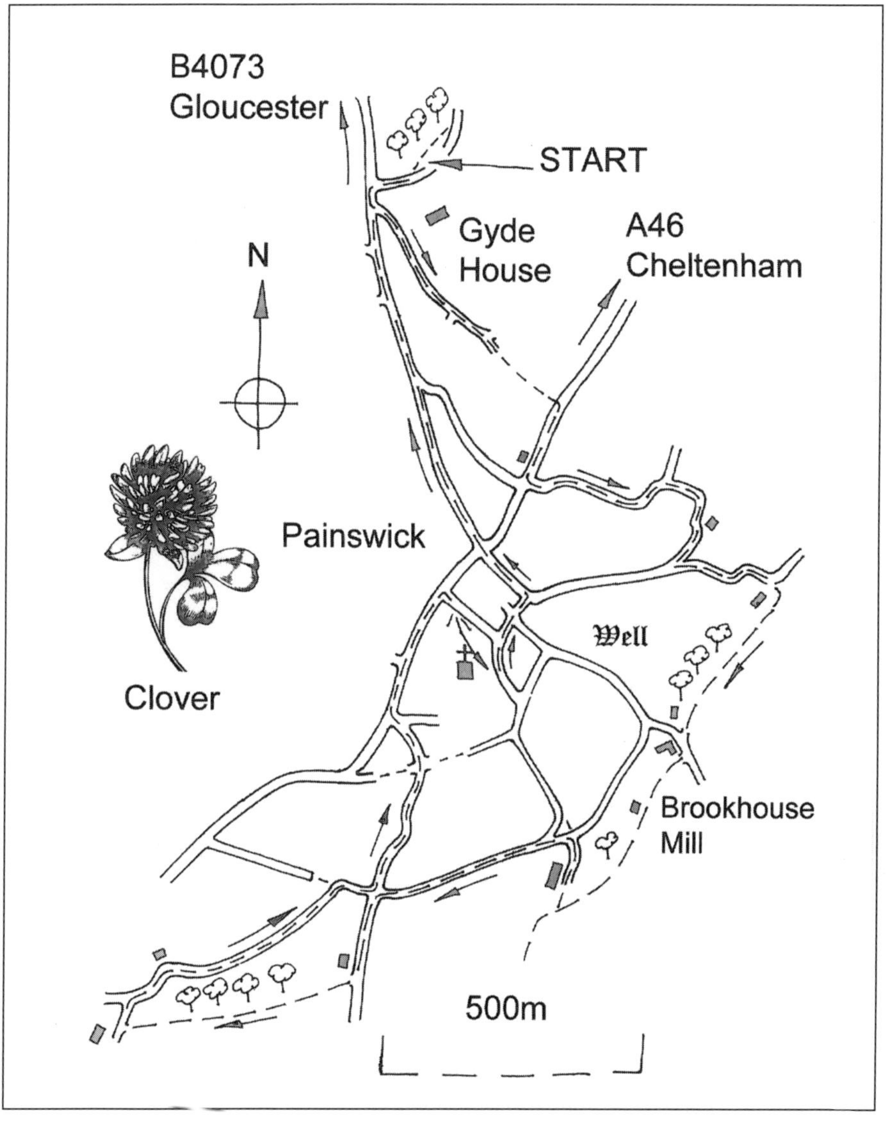

✓The island in the middle of the pond is a favourite nesting place for swans. Baby swans are fluffy and grey to begin with but then develop brown feathers. These begin to be replaced by white ones after about a year.

Q4 What is a baby swan called?

Walk up to the road junction and turn left. After about 400m you arrive at a cross-roads. Pause by the post box on the left.

✓Can you see that the post box has the letters VR on it? This stands for Victoria Regina, which means that this post box was made when Queen Victoria was on the throne.

Q5 Most post boxes now have ER on them. What do you think the E stands for?

(*To cut the walk short, turn right here and walk up this steep road. Pick up the directions again where shown* *.)

To continue with the walk, turn left into Stepping Stones Lane. This was the main route in from Stroud until the turnpike road (now the A46) was built around 1820. At the bottom of the hill is The Little Bridge House which was built on the site of Springs Mill. Immediately after crossing the river take a footpath on the right. After squeezing between two evergreen hedgerows it passes between some young **lime** trees to reach a meadow.

Follow the path along the right hand side of the field which soon passes a solitary **oak** tree.

Q6 What is the seed of the oak tree called?

✓If you are walking in spring or summer you may see daisies growing here. They were once used to help heal injuries. They would be crushed by the sackful and bandages would be soaked in the juice to help wounds to heal more quickly. Also look out for the mauve or cream coloured clover which grows quite close to the ground. Their leaves grow in groups of three. See if you can find a clover with four leaves. If you do, keep it - it means you are going to be very lucky!

At the end of the field, cross a stile and a footbridge to reach Kings Mill. Turn right here and walk up the drive to a lane. Turn right again, and follow this lane to the road junction where you saw the old post-box. Turn left now, and walk up a steep road.

* After a lengthy climb you reach the main road through the town. Turn right here and walk past a car park lined with **beech** trees. Soon you arrive at the gabled entrance to the church yard.

Q7 How many bells are carved into the wood around the roof?

Stay with the road until you reach the end of the churchyard where you turn right into Victoria Square. Head for the churchyard entrance, but before you enter, look left at the Town Hall.

Q8 When was the Town Hall built? (Clue: look up near the roof.)

Enter the churchyard, and take the middle of the three paths through the yew trees. Beyond the church, go straight on into St Mary's Street and turn left to see the spectacle stocks.

✓A long time ago these were used to punish criminals. They would sit on the stone seat and their legs would be fitted through the round holes and locked in place. They might be left here for days. Is this worse than the 'naughty step'?

Carry on along St Mary's street, passing by the public conveniences to reach Cardynham House at The Cross.

✓*Look right here.*

Q9 Down the road there used to be a pub called the Golden ....

Go straight on at The Cross, passing another of Painswick's old pubs, The Royal Oak Inn. Turn left at the road junction and climb up Bisley Street, which was once the main road through the town. Look out for Byfield House and its 13th century door.

✓This cottage was once home to a weaver, someone who made wool into cloth. The wool would arrive on the back of a donkey, so this old door had to be wide enough for the donkey to get into the house with all the wool still on its back!

Carry on up to the cross-roads and go straight across into Gloucester Street. A weather vane can be seen high up on a house on the left.

✓Knowing wind direction was part of primitive mans' survival kit. It enabled him to stay downwind of an animal he was hunting so the animal wouldn't pick up his scent. It was also useful in battle. With the wind behind him an archer would be able to fire his arrows further than the archers in the opposing army. It also helped sailors in the days when boats were powered by sails.

Continue up Gloucester Street until it reaches a road junction. Go straight on here, noting the old animal pound on the left which was once used to collect stray or missing farm animals. After about 50m, cross the road to see an old milepost.

✓Years ago, mileposts were placed by the side of the road so that people knew how far they still had to travel. This one has Roman numbers.

Q10 If V is five and I is one, can you guess how many miles it might be to Gloucester?

Continue away from the town until you reach Golf Course Road and the start of the walk.

Painswick Checklist

☐	Red telephone box	☐	Horse
☐	Round window	☐	Swan
☐	Nesting box	☐	Stone ball
☐	Fallen tree	☐	Wheeley bin
☐	Duck	☐	A racehorse (maybe not a real one!)

Walk 16. Daglingworth

Daglingworth and the Duntisbournes, are sleepy stone built villages hidden in the Dunt valley. They're largely undiscovered, so enjoy their subtle charms while the rest the world thunders by on the nearby A417 trunk road. The stream crosses the road in a couple of places to create idyllic spots for tired little feet to have a paddle - come prepared!

Distance	5km (3 miles)
Starting point	Leave the A417 where signposted Stratton, Daglingworth, Bagendon and Perrots Brook. Follow the signs for Daglingworth, and when you drop down into the village turn left signposted Cirencester. After 400m, turn right into Lower End and after 100m park on the roadside verge opposite Brook House. Grid Reference: 997048 Postcode: GL7 7AH
Short cut	The easiest way to cut the walk short is to turn back at Duntisbourne Rouse and return by the same route
Terrain	Undulating walk over field paths and minor roads
Public toilets	None
Refreshments	None, apart from dipping your toes in the river!
Pushchairs	None
Leaf collection	Oak, ash, beech and sycamore
Map	OS Explorer Map 168

Daglingworth and the Duntisbournes

The most notable feature of Daglingworth church are the four Saxon carvings, set into the walls of the nave and aisle. They were found hidden in the chancel arch and because of this are wonderfully well preserved.

There is hardly a village to speak of at Middle Duntisbourne, but it has a delightful ford with a vintage tractor permanently moored in it.

Duntisbourne Rouse is hardly any bigger but it does have a wonderful church. Even here, in an area blessed with more than its fair share of charming village churches, this is a gem. Alec Clifton-Taylor in his book *The English Parish Church as A Work of Art* describes it as one of his favourite churches in the whole of England. A mixture of Saxon and Norman, its charm lies in its simplicity, and from the evidence of its worn stone floor it has been popular throughout the ages.

It contains a surprise, made possible by the steeply sloping ground. Tucked under the chancel is a tiny chapel which feels incredibly old. The low vaulted room is lit in the morning by a shaft of sunlight which streams in through a tiny window in the east wall.

The village ford is situated on a no through road, so nothing spoils the enjoyment of the pond skaters or the butterflies, which perform their timeless dance above the rushes.

Saint Michael's Duntisbourne Rouse

The Walk

With Brook House on your right, walk up the hill until the lane bends left. Here you turn right to find a path which leads to a field. Walk along the field margin under the shade of newly planted **oak** trees.

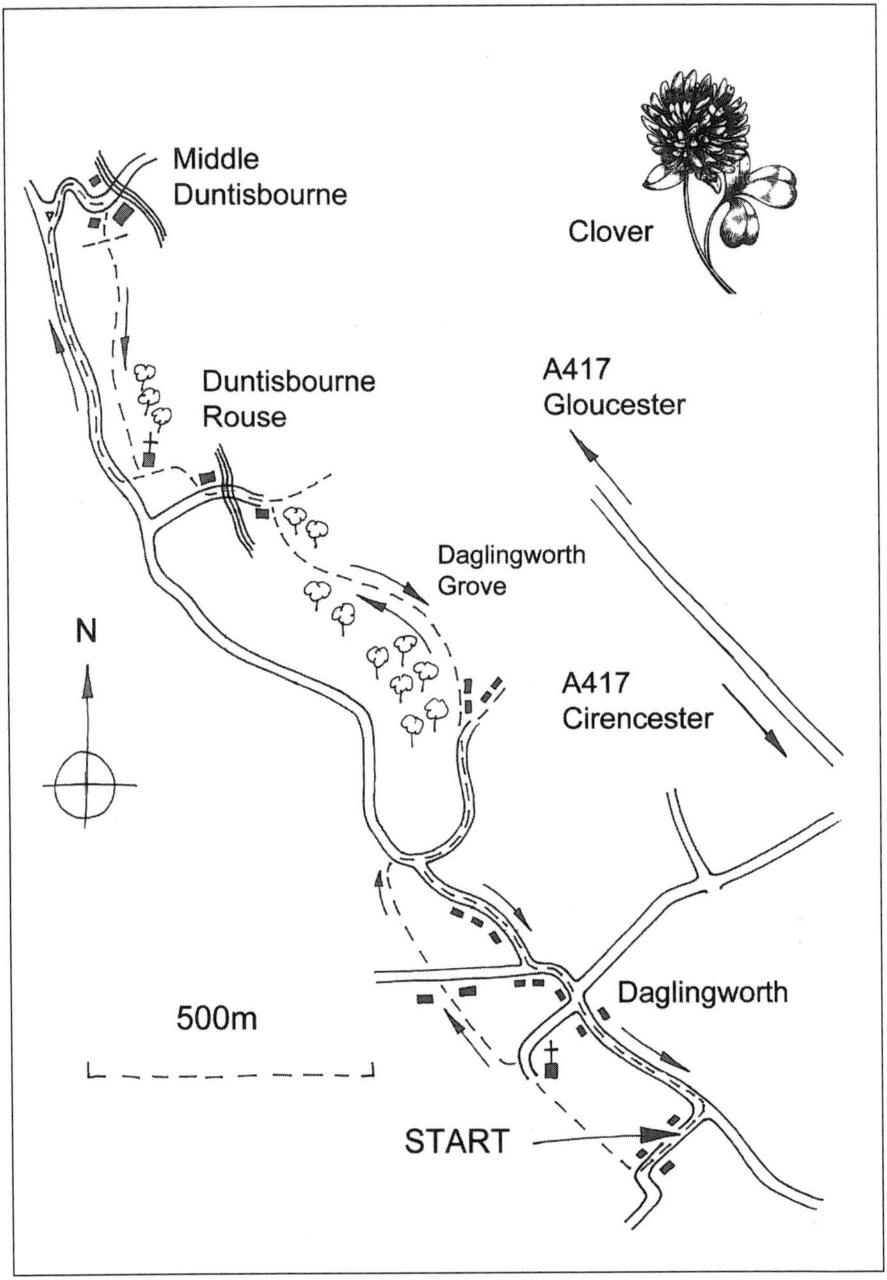
Middle
Duntisbourne
Clover
A417
Gloucester
Duntisbourne
Rouse
Daglingworth
Grove
N
A417
Cirencester
Daglingworth
500m
START

✓Note that a fence that has been placed around each tree. This is to protect the tree from deer as they love to eat the bark of young trees. Trees can die if too much bark is damaged.

Q1 What is the seed of an oak tree called?

After passing through a gate, the path becomes a track which soon reaches Daglingworth Church.

✓Have you heard the church bells yet? The bells are found in the belfry, which is near the top of the church tower behind some windows that have no glass in them. Instead, there are stone strips, which allow the sound of the bells to come out but stop the wind and rain from getting in. Bats like to live up in the belfry. A bat is a bit like a flying mouse. They sleep during the day and come out at night to eat insects. Bats have big appetites because flying uses up lots of energy. The tiny pipistrelle bat will eat over 3,000 insects in a night!

Q2 Does the pipstrelle bat weigh about the same as a pound coin or a mobile phone?

As the road bends right near a converted barn, look for a stile on the left near a farm gate. After this, follow a fenced path past a weather vane to reach a stone stile.

Q3 What can you see on top of the weathervane?

Cross the field, aiming for a conifer standing between two distant cottages. Follow the wall under the conifer to reach a road. Cross the road and climb some steps opposite to reach a path which squeezes between a wall and a hedge. Soon you reach a road where you turn right and then left onto a 'No Through Road' (you will be returning this way later).

Shortly the tarmac finishes near a power line, where you fork left onto a stony path which climbs up behind some cottages. After passing through a gate, follow a path along the left hand side of a field. This passes under the shade of some **ash** trees, which reach over from the woodland on the left. This is an ideal spot to leave the children a treat for the return journey (see 'lets make walking fun!').

✓In spring look into the woods to see the bluebells. In summer, see if you can find the flowers of the clover (see map) which grow quite close to the ground.

They will either be pink or cream coloured, and their leaves grow in groups of three. See if you can find a clover with four leaves. If you do, keep it - it means you are going to be very lucky!

At the end of the field, pass through a farm gate shaded by a magnificent **beech** tree.

✓ Look under the beech tree and see if you can see any empty nutshells. Squirrels love to eat beech nuts, but when there are too many they bury them so that they have something to eat during the winter. They must have a good memory to be able to find them again! Could you survive as a squirrel? We will be coming back this way later so bury some nutshells and see if you can find them on the way back!

Beyond the gate, follow the wall for 30m and then walk down the pasture aiming for a gate to the right of a cottage. After a second gate, turn left onto a path which drops down from the right. This soon becomes a track as it approaches the ford at Duntibourne Rous.

✓Look at the water and see if there are any insects running about on the surface. Water has a thin 'skin' which can support the weight of an insect. Look how the insects' legs push down on the surface of the water.

Q4 How many legs does an insect have?

Immediately after Chucklestone Cottage, turn right onto a footpath near a wooden door. This soon reaches the churchyard of St Michael's Duntisbourne Rous. The secret chapel is found down some steps on this side of the church. Pause below the sundial above the church door.

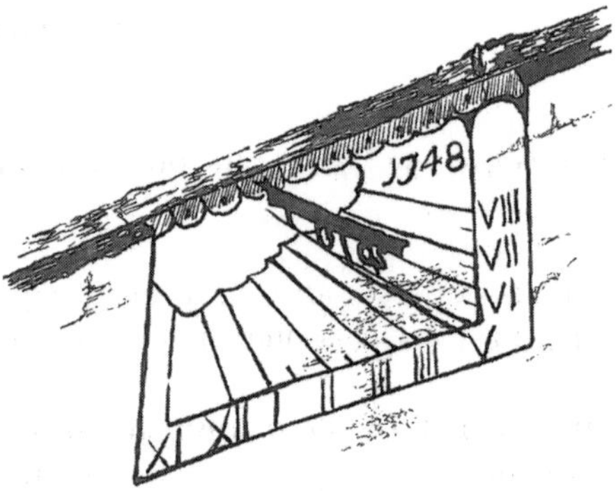

✓Long ago, clocks were very expensive, and people used a sundial instead. The angled metal arm casts a shadow on the wall and as the sun moves across the sky the shadow moves allowing you to tell the time. At midday, the sun is directly overhead, and your shadow is very short. If the sun is out, mark the length of your shadow on the ground with a couple of twigs or flowers. You will be coming back this way later and you will be able to tell if your shadow has got longer or shorter.

Q5 Can you see the date on the sundial?

Walk to the left of the church and leave the churchyard along a short path which soon reaches a road. Turn right here and follow the road until it reaches a road junction.

✓This road can get a bit icy in winter and there are buckets of grit along the road. Grit stops cars from sliding on the ice. As you walk along the road, see how many buckets you can find.

At the road junction turn right, but before you walk down the hill, look at the post box on the right.

✓Can you see that it has the letters 'VR' on it? This stands for Victoria Regina, which means that it was made in Victorian times. The postman would have collected the mail using a horse and cart. Maybe the post box was put here to save him from taking his horse and cart down the hill into the village. Queen Victoria died in 1901.

Q6 How many letters were posted **every day** in 1901? 1 million, 3 million, or 6 million?

✓Did you find all seven grit buckets?

Walk down into Middle Duntisbourne and its ford. Just before the ford, look over your right shoulder for a path that passes between a cottage and a barn. This is your route, but before you continue with the walk, wander over to the footbridge next to the ford.

✓Can you see what looks like a rule sticking out of the water near the bridge? This is a depth gauge, and if it has been raining heavily there could be quite a lot of water flowing across the road. This gauge will help motorists decide if the water is shallow enough to drive through.

Q7 What is the maximum depth on the gauge?

Return to the path, and follow it up to a stile from which you aim for a tree on the skyline. As you reach the tree, continue across a grassy track and follow a path alongside a wall. This soon reaches a stile after passing through some saplings. Beyond the stile, cross a narrow strip of land to reach a metal gate. Maintain your bearing over the crest of the hill in front of you, and drop down the other side to reach a rickety stile in the far corner of the field.

The path continues along the bottom of a steep sided meadow before climbing up to a stile on the edge of some woodland.

✓This meadow is full of flowers in summer. Look out for the meadow cranesbill which grows about half a metre tall. They are easy to spot because their blue/violet flowers have five petals. Also look out for the knapweed, a purple flower which looks like a thistle but without the prickles.

Follow the path through the woods which are carpeted with bluebell and wild garlic in spring.

✓Wild garlic has long smooth leaves and white flowers. Rub the leaves between your fingers. They should smell of garlic!

Ignore a gate on the right and stay with the path which keeps to the left of a fence before returning you to the churchyard you left earlier. Walk to the right of the church and then turn left onto the churchyard path.

✓ If the sun is still out, go to where you stood earlier and see if your shadow is any longer or shorter than it was before.

Q8 If you are walking in the afternoon would you expect your shadow to get longer or shorter?

Walk down the hill and out of the churchyard. You are re-tracing the route you walked earlier so when you reach the road, turn left and re-cross the ford. After this, turn right just after Woodside Cottage and after passing through two gates, climb back up the pasture to the farm gate under the beech tree.

✓Can you remember where you buried the nut shells?

Q9 You are most likely to see a grey squirrel. What other kind of squirrel lives in this country?

✓Do your fingers still smell of wild garlic?

Walk back along the edge of the field and behind the cottages to reach the road down to Daglingworth. At the road junction, turn left and head into the village. At the road junction near the telephone box turn left, and follow the road round a right hand bend. Beyond Woodside Cottage, climb up onto a road-side path shaded by **sycamore** and **ash**. When this finishes, turn right into Lower End to reach the start of the walk.

Daglingworth Checklist

☐ Stone ball	☐ Tractor
☐ Dog (maybe not a real one!)	☐ Telephone box
☐ Round window	☐ Post box
☐ Cow or a sheep	☐ Wheeley bin
☐ Grit bucket	

Walk 17. Uley

Uley is attractive Cotswold village with an interesting history, much of which is explored on this walk. This hilly route also includes magnificent views, leafy glades, grassy meadows, a prehistoric fort and even a working brewery!

Distance	**5km (3 miles)**
Starting point	**Uley is four miles east of Dursley and is best approached from this direction along the B4066. Enter the village after rounding a left hand bend and park immediately beyond a cross roads, in a small car-park next to a bus stop.** **Grid Reference: 786979 Postcode: GL11 5TE**
Short cut	**Yes, see text and dotted route on map**
Terrain	**Grassy paths, pavements and steep woodland tracks which may become muddy after rain**
Public toilets	**None apart from those available to the patrons of The Old Crown**
Refreshments	**The Old Crown Inn**
Pushchairs	**Not suitable**
Leaf collection	**Oak, ash and beech**
Map	**OS Explorer Map 168**

Uley

It was Uley's iron-age inhabitants who constructed the great hill fort above the village. Known as Uley Bury, this 32 acre earthwork commands a spectacular view over the Severn Vale and is the finest of its kind in Gloucestershire.

Uley was a cloth village. It was internationally famous for its blue cloth, which could be found in the uniforms of both sides in the battle of Waterloo. Sadly all this came to an abrupt end with the bankruptcy of Sheppards Mill in 1837. The impact on Uley and the surrounding area was immediate and catastrophic. At a stroke, 1,000 people lost their livelihoods. There was no other employment, and by the following year 84% of the population of the parish were officially paupers. Some went to Merthyr Tydfil, which was then the iron making capital of the world, but many left for the New World. Not surprisingly, they missed the sheltered valley they would never see again. In 1837, Moses Bendle Garlick, a weaver from Uley, left for Australia and settled just north of what is currently Adelaide. He named the settlement Uleybury.

Today, Uley enjoys a quiet prosperity in an undiscovered corner of the Cotswolds. The legacy of its cloth weaving days are the elegant Georgian and Queen Anne style clothiers houses and the mills, some of which survive as private houses.

The walk

Walk back to the cross-roads and turn left into Lampern Hill. Pause by 'The Shears', a nicely finished garage!

✓ Look up at the weather vane. Knowing wind direction was important when man had to hunt to survive. It enabled him to stay downwind of an animal he was hunting so the animal wouldn't pick up his scent. Later it was useful in battle. With the wind behind him an archer would be able to fire his arrows further than the archers in the opposing army. Look out for more weather vanes later.

Q1 What animal stands on top of the weather vane?

Carry on past 'The Shears' but cross to the other side of the road in readiness for the blind left hand bend you are now approaching. Follow the road up round to the left and, just after passing the entrance to 'Stout's Hill', turn left into the driveway of Dauncey's Mill. Ignore the gateway to the 'Walled Garden', and walk down towards the wooden gates of the mill.

Bear right at the gates and follow a path alongside a wall. Only the clock tower can be seen of this mill, parts of which date back to 1689.

Q2 What can you see on the weather vane on top of the clock tower?

Pass through the kissing gate and walk along the left hand side of the field.

✓*Look out for the mauve or cream coloured clover which grows quite close to the ground. Their leaves grow in groups of three. See if you can find a clover* with four leaves. If you do, keep it - it means you are going to be very lucky! See Daglingworth map for picture.

Go straight on at the end of this field, ignoring a footbridge on the left. Pass through two more fields and drop down to a footbridge at the end of the second.

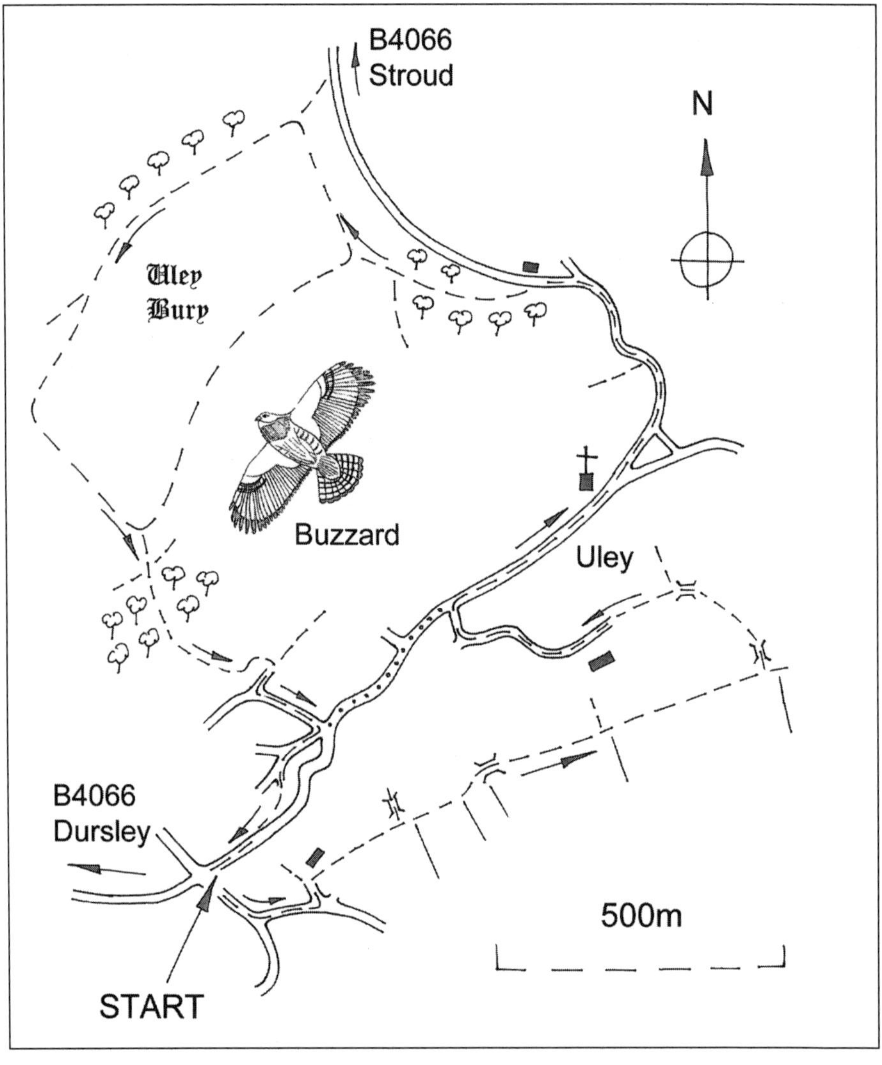

Walk to the end of the next field, where you ignore a gate on the left and go straight on using a stile next to a gap in the fence. At the end of the next field turn left onto an old stone bridge.

✓ Look at how worn this bridge is. 200 years ago there was a mill near here (a kind of factory) which employed many local people. They would have walked to work from the villages behind you. There were so many of them, and they crossed this bridge for so many years, that they wore it away in the middle.

Beyond the footbridge bear slightly left, and cross the field to find a stile and another footbridge on its left hand boundary. Climb up the next field, aiming just to the right of a house with two tall chimneys to find a stile next to a gate. After this, walk along a grassy track which soon becomes a metalled road.

You are now approaching Sheppards Mill, once famous for its blue cloth. At its peak it was a complex of 30 buildings, but now only three remain, all in residential use. Down to the left is the 'Great Mill' and the nearby 'Clerks House', while ahead of you is the 'Press House', where the final stage in the cloth making process took place. The mill owner built himself Gatcombe Park, now the home of Princess Anne, but died before it was completed. After the mill closed in 1837, it had a number of uses before being converted into a dwelling in the 1980s.

Continue along the road into the village. After passing the old chapel the road bends right to reach the main road. Turn right here and pause by the old petrol station. (*A left turn here takes you back to the start. Follow the pavement until it finishes near Court House, and go straight on into Lampern View. Pick up the directions again where shown* *.)

✓ Many village petrol stations would have looked like this 50 years ago.

Q3 What is the name of the petrol company?

Cross the road and walk past the post office to find a raised pavement which leads up to the churchyard gate. Pause by the plaque on the right hand pillar.

✓ This plaque remembers the wedding of Lady Diana (mother of Prince William and Prince Harry) to Prince Charles.

Q4 What year did they get married?

Walk into the churchyard and turn right at the church door. Follow the path out of the church yard.

The petrol station at Uley

Q5 What is the name of the pub across the road?

Follow the road out of the village. Soon you come to an old post box.

✓ Look at the letters ER on the post box. These letters stand for Edward Rex which means that this post box was made when King Edward V11 was on the throne. He ruled between 1901 and 1910. The roman number 7 (VII) helps us work this out.

Q6 On most post boxes the letters ER stand for a different monarch. Who might this be?

Stay with the road-side path until it ends near a bus stop. You have a walk of about 50m along this road with a blind bend behind you, so take care over this section. Look for a cottage on the right hand side of the road and just as you pass it, look left for a path that climbs steeply up through the trees. Fork right after 30m and walk up this steep path.

✓ Let's go back 2,000 years to when an iron age fort existed at the top of this hill. You are a member of the Dobunni tribe and everyone in your village is talking about an attack by a neighbouring tribe. You are going to climb up to the hill fort because you will be safe there.

At the top of the woods, pass through a gate and bear right, ignoring a gate on the left.

✓ Up ahead of you would have been two wooden walls with a ditch in front of each wall.

Climb up through the ditches and ramparts of the fort, and bear right when the path levels out beyond a way-mark post and a small **oak** tree.

✓ You are now safe behind the walls! There would have been spears, swords and axes leaning against the wall for protection.

Uley Bury was built on an outlier of the Cotswold escarpment, and is a natural defensive position with four distinct corners. Follow the path to the first corner where you turn left near a display board.

A variety of trees have colonised the slope to the right including **oak**, **ash** and **beech.**

✓ This hill is a popular place to see buzzards, which soar on the warm air rising from the valley bottom. They fly without flapping their wings so they are quite easy to spot. There's a picture of a buzzard on the map.

Follow the path to the second corner and turn left again.

✓ Can you see why forts were built on hill tops? You could see your enemies coming and by the time they struggled to the top they would be quite tired. 2,000 years ago there would have been far more trees in the valley, but you knew where the enemy tribe were because the smoke from their camp fires would be rising up through the trees.

At the third corner look for a sunken path near a way mark post. Turn right onto this, and follow the stony path down to a gate at the edge of a wood. Walk down through the trees to reach a stile at the top of a field. Beyond this walk down to a metalled path that reaches up from the village. At the bottom of this turn right, and cross a stile next to a farm gate to reach a track. At the end of this turn left onto a back lane and follow this down into the village.

Soon you pass the Uley Brewery on the left.

Q7 The brewery has a weathervane on it. Can you see what animal stands on top?
Q8 Look carefully at the wooden window. When was the brewery built?

This building started its life as Price's Brewery. For a time the building fell into disrepair but after a period of restoration it opened as the Uley Brewery in 1985.

At the bottom of the road turn sharp right into Lampern View.

* After 50m fork left, and left again after another 50m, to reach a path that takes you to the main road. Ignore the steps down to this, and stay on the high path which passes one of Uley's former pubs before reaching the start of the walk.

Q9 What is the name of the pub?

Uley Checklist

☐ Round window	☐ Fallen tree
☐ Clock face	☐ Garden shed
☐ Someone walking a dog	☐ Beer barrel
☐ Satellite dish	☐ Wheeley bin
☐ Post box	

Walk 18. Northleach

A delightful walk between an old wool town and Hampnett, a village high on the hill and pure Cotswold in character. Grown-ups will appreciate the magnificent 'wool' church and the medieval market place with its charming half timbered Tudor houses. Children will enjoy the museum of mechanical instruments, the 'Dolls House Shop' and the old prison, where a vacant cell can always be found for a naughty little person!

Distance	**6km (3.75 miles)**
Starting point	**Approaching Northleach from the east, leave the A40 where signposted 'Northleach Town' and follow the road in. Immediately after passing Eastington Road (signposted Eastington and Aldsworth), park on the left hand side of the road. Grid Reference: 118144 Postcode: GL54 3PH**
Short cut	**The most convenient place to cut the walk short would be to turn back when you reach the traffic lights near the old prison**
Terrain	**Undulating walk over fields, quiet lanes and pavements. There may be cattle**
Public toilets	**In the Market Place**
Refreshments	**There are a number of pubs in the town**
Pushchairs	**Not suitable**
Leaf collection	**Sycamore, lime, willow and ash**
Map	**OS Explorer Map OL45**

Northleach

Northleach is named after the River Leach, which rises in nearby Hampnett, a rural idyll nestling among the trees at the top of a valley. The town itself is renowned for having a workhouse at one end and a prison at the other. In between stand some fine medieval houses and the magnificent 'wool' church of St Peter and St Paul, embellished in the 15th century by the town's rich wool merchants. Between 1340 and 1540, Northleach prospered as a centre of the wool trade and the language of every European country could be heard in its crowded streets. The export of raw fleeces was banned by an act of parliament in the early 16th century and Northleach, whose stream was not powerful enough to drive a mill, was left behind in the rush from raw wool to manufactured cloth. The town's economy collapsed almost overnight, and it became a small market town which people hurried through on the way to somewhere else.

It enjoyed a temporary revival in the 18th and 19th centuries when it took on a new role as a coaching centre, until this trade too was lost to the railways. Northleach was again condemned to period in the wilderness. In 1867 the *British Medical Journal* reported: "Its occupation is now wholly gone, a more trade-forsaken town we have never seen, even its jail is empty, and seems, from its wide-barred eyes, wistfully looking for the felons that never come where there is nothing to steal". Grass was growing down the middle of the High Street, and many properties were vacant or derelict. Only the tumbleweed was missing.

The church at Northleach

Its position on the main road between Gloucester and London meant that when the motor car arrived the town enjoyed something of a revival, but the parallel growth of heavy goods traffic hindered its development. Northleach recoiled with its hands over its ears against the sound of heavy goods vehicles thundering through the market square. Relief came with the building of the M4 motorway and more recently the eagerly awaited bypass, which had been discussed since the 1930s.

For many years the name Northleach was synonymous with decline, but today's town has recovered some of its former energy and supports a thriving local community. Shops and pubs are plentiful and attractions like 'Keith Harding's World of Mechanical Music' and the 'Dolls House Shop' make for an interesting afternoon with the family.

The walk

✓We are going to find out what it was like to live in the countryside in Victorian times.

Across the road, hiding shamefully behind the trees is Northleach Court, which was once a workhouse.

✓In Victorian times this was a workhouse. It was a place your family came to live if they were homeless. This could easily happen if your father was taken ill and unable to work. It was a place to be scared of because you would be separated from other members of your family and you would sleep in a room full of strangers. You would have your hair cut short and would have to wear a uniform. It wasn't very clean and you could easily die from a disease like measles.

Q1 Can you see when it was built? (Clue: look between the windows.)
Q2 If you had measles, what would your skin be covered in?

Head into the town centre along 'East End' to a point where the road joggles to reach the Market Place. You will be returning this way, but for now bear left into 'The Peep', which passes under a Sycamore tree to reach 'The Green'. Go straight on through this small parking area, and follow the road beyond round a tight left hand bend. After 50m turn right into 'Church Walk' and stay with this until it bends right to reach the churchyard gate.

✓Have you heard the church bells yet? The bells are found in the belfry which

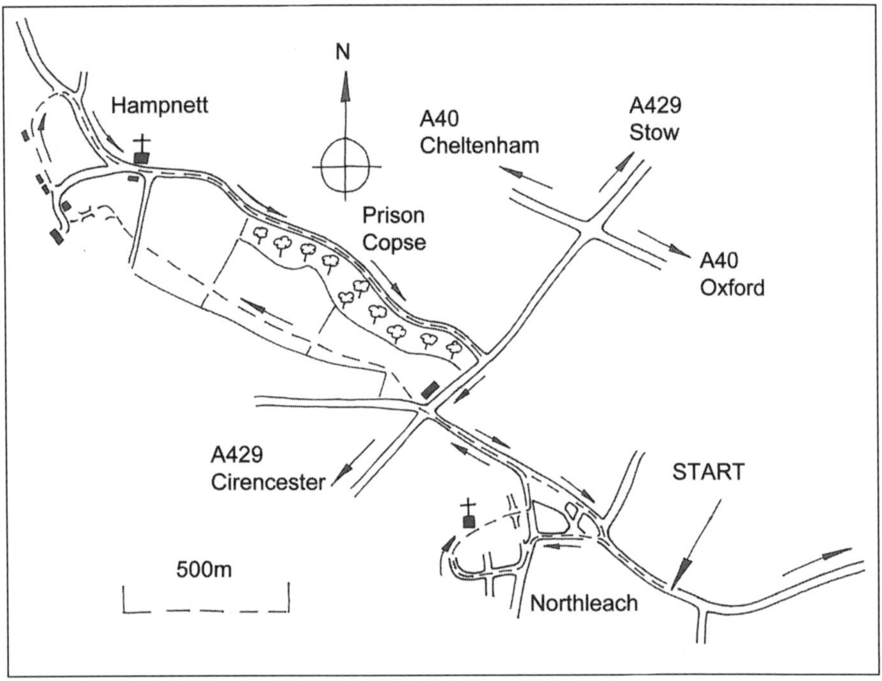

is near the top of the church tower behind some windows that have no glass in them. Instead there are wooden strips which allow the sound of the bells to come out but stop the wind and rain from getting in. Bats like to live up in the belfry. A bat is a bit like a flying mouse. They sleep during the day and come out at night to eat insects.

Q3 What can you see on top of the church?

Follow path to the right of the church and leave the churchyard through a gate. Continue straight on to the 'Market Place' and turn left to reach the war memorial. Turn left here and walk along 'West End', which was once the A40 trunk road before the bypass was built in the 1980s.

Q4 What can you see on top of the clock?

After passing some **lime** trees, cross the road and walk towards the traffic lights. Go straight on here and look for a stile on the right which leads into a field. Bear left, and walk down towards the end of a ditch which finishes at the corner of a field. Follow the path down the left hand side of this field to find a farm gate next to a wall. From here, continue to the end of the next field to find a gate near a water trough.

✓Cows use this water trough to drink out of. It may be a bit muddy here because they are messy drinkers! They can drink as much as a bath full of water every day. See if you can see their footprints near the trough. They have big footprints with two 'toes'.

Q5 What is a baby cow called?

Continue through a crop field, and after crossing a concrete track, walk across some rough pasture to reach a gate 30m to the left of a pole-mounted transformer. Walk into the trees, and follow a stony path past a lake and alongside a wall. This soon reaches some rough ground which is crossed to find a bridge and some steps leading up to a driveway. Turn right here and follow the road to a right turn, where you go straight on between some cottages and willow trees to reach a gate. Now, using the wall on the left as a guide, go straight across the rough ground, aiming for a hedge and a cottage in the middle distance. Beyond this, pass the old school room to reach a farm gate.

✓This building used to be the village school and there was only one classroom. All the children were taught together. Imagine being in the same class as your brother or sister! Sometimes you were too busy working in the fields to go to school, especially if it was harvest time. There was no electricity, so the windows had to be big to let in lots of light.

Q6 How many windows are there?

After this, bear slightly right to reach a gate next to a cattle grid. Walk down to Hampnett village green and turn right. Follow the road past the source of the River Leach until you reach a post box with 'V.R.' on it.

✓'V.R.' stands for 'Victoria Regina' which means that this post box was made when Queen Victoria was on the throne. In Victorian times the cottages would have been smaller and the gardens would have been used to grow vegetables. Everyone would have kept animals like a pig or a few chickens. If you were born in this village you would spend your whole life working in the surrounding fields and would never think of moving away. There was no electricity; you found your way to bed by the light of a candle. You wore clothes that your older brother or sister had grown too big for.

Q7 Most post boxes now have the letters 'E.R.' on them. What does the 'E' stand for?

Opposite the church stands an old barn, now converted into a large house.

✓This was once a barn. A big building used to store crops so that they stayed dry during the winter. It's a house now but you can still see the big wooden barn door. The crop was harvested and brought into the barn on the back of a cart pulled by a horse. This is why the door is so big.

Q8 What might the cart be pulled by now?

Hampnett Parish church dates back to the Norman period, and its interior was elaborately decorated in 1868. The effect is startling, and gives an impression of what the church may have looked like in medieval times.

Continue along the road.

✓You may see crops growing in the fields near the road. Crops are cut down and removed from the field using a machine. This is called harvesting. In Victorian times crops were cut down using a scythe, a kind of long knife. It would then be gathered into a bundle and thrown onto a cart which would take it to the barn. The whole family (including you!) would get up as soon as it was light to harvest the crop. It was such a big task that you could be there until it got dark. After that you worked using the light of the moon. It was very hard work and you got so tired you fell asleep eating your supper!

Q9 What is the name of a machine used to harvest crops? .... Harvester

Continue along the road, which passes under the shade of **ash** trees, to reach a road junction. Turn right here, and walk down to the Old Prison which dates back to 1791. Admission is free and you can see the cells, the courtroom and an exhibition of agricultural implements and wagons.

✓In Victorian times you could go to prison for quite minor offences like stealing firewood or chickens. When it was first opened, the prisoners could earn a little money, making baskets and woollen thread. When they were released they could keep half of what they earned. In 1827 things got harder. A treadmill was installed, a bit like a gerbils' exercise wheel, except you could never get off. It was a bit like having to climb up the stairs all day long, and by the time they went to bed they might have climbed over 3,000 metres.

Turn left at the traffic lights and follow the road back through the town. Go straight on at the Market Place and pass between the 'Dolls House Shop' and the 'Mechanical Music Museum' to reach 'East End'. Follow this road back to the start of the walk.

Northleach Checklist

- ☐ Stone ball
- ☐ Telephone box
- ☐ Round window
- ☐ Cow
- ☐ Clock
- ☐ Water trough
- ☐ Wheeley bin
- ☐ Burglar alarm
- ☐ Post box

Walk 19. Duntisbourne Abbots

Leave the tourists behind and follow the infant river Dunt through two idyllic Cotswold villages. You may never have been here before but the villages are strangely familiar, having been seen anonymously on biscuit tin lids and jigsaws. There are plenty of opportunities for a paddle so come prepared!

Distance	6km (3.75 miles)
Starting point	Leave the A417 Gloucester to Cirencester trunk road near the Highwayman Inn signposted Syde, Winstone and Elkstone. Follow the signs to Winstone and after about 1km you arrive at the village. As the road makes a sharp right hand bend, turn left into Notch Road and park on the roadside verge just outside the village. Grid Reference: 964096 Postcode: GL7 7JU
Short cut	None
Terrain	Undulating country lanes, old tracks and grassy paths
Public toilets	None
Refreshments	None apart from the sparkling river Dunt!
Pushchairs	Not suitable
Leaf collection	Ash, beech and sycamore
Map	OS Explorer Map 179

The Walk

Walk back into the village and at the road junction turn left into Back Lane. Walk down to the next junction where you turn right. After walking down past the Old School, the road climbs up to another junction where you go straight on. Shortly you arrive at Winstone Baptist Chapel. Look at the sign on its wall advertising the Sunday school.

✓Sunday schools were started by the church at a time when there was no education for most children. They had to work alongside their parents for six days a week in factories or fields - sometimes as much as 12 hours a day. Children were not forced to go to Sunday school, but by 1831 a quarter of all children were attending because it was the only way they could learn to read and write. It was the beginning of state education.

Q1 What time did Sunday school start?

Continue away from the village, eventually following the road round a sharp left hand bend. Ignore a right turn to Caudle Green, and go straight on, passing to the left of Gaskills Farm.

After about 300m turn left onto a permissive path signposted Duntisbourne Abbots. Pass through an electric gate shaded by an **ash** tree, and walk past Ashgrove Farm and its stable block. Have a look at the weathervane on the stable.

✓Weathervanes tell us the direction of the wind. In ancient times this was important if you were out hunting animals. If the wind was behind you the deer would pick up your scent and run away. Also, if there was a storm in the distance you would be able to tell if it was coming towards you.

Q2 What can you see on the weathervane?

Leave the tarmac behind and continue along a sandy path, which is soon accompanied by a hedgerow.

✓The hedgerow on the left makes an ideal place for small animals to take shelter and for birds to make their nests. You should be able to see hawthorn with its sharp thorns and small red berries. Also, the prickly stems of bramble which give us blackberries in late summer. These are all eaten during the winter, when their bright colours make them easily found by hungry birds and animals. Further on you might see the prickly leaves of the holly bush that we see at Christmas. Horses sometimes use this path; can you see the tell-tale signs?

Soon you pass to the left of Longfurlong Barn, after which the path broadens out to become a farm track. This climbs up past a copse with its mix of deciduous and evergreen trees.

✓Deciduous trees lose their leaves in the autumn but evergreens keep them all year round. The conifers near the path are evergreen trees and their needle-like

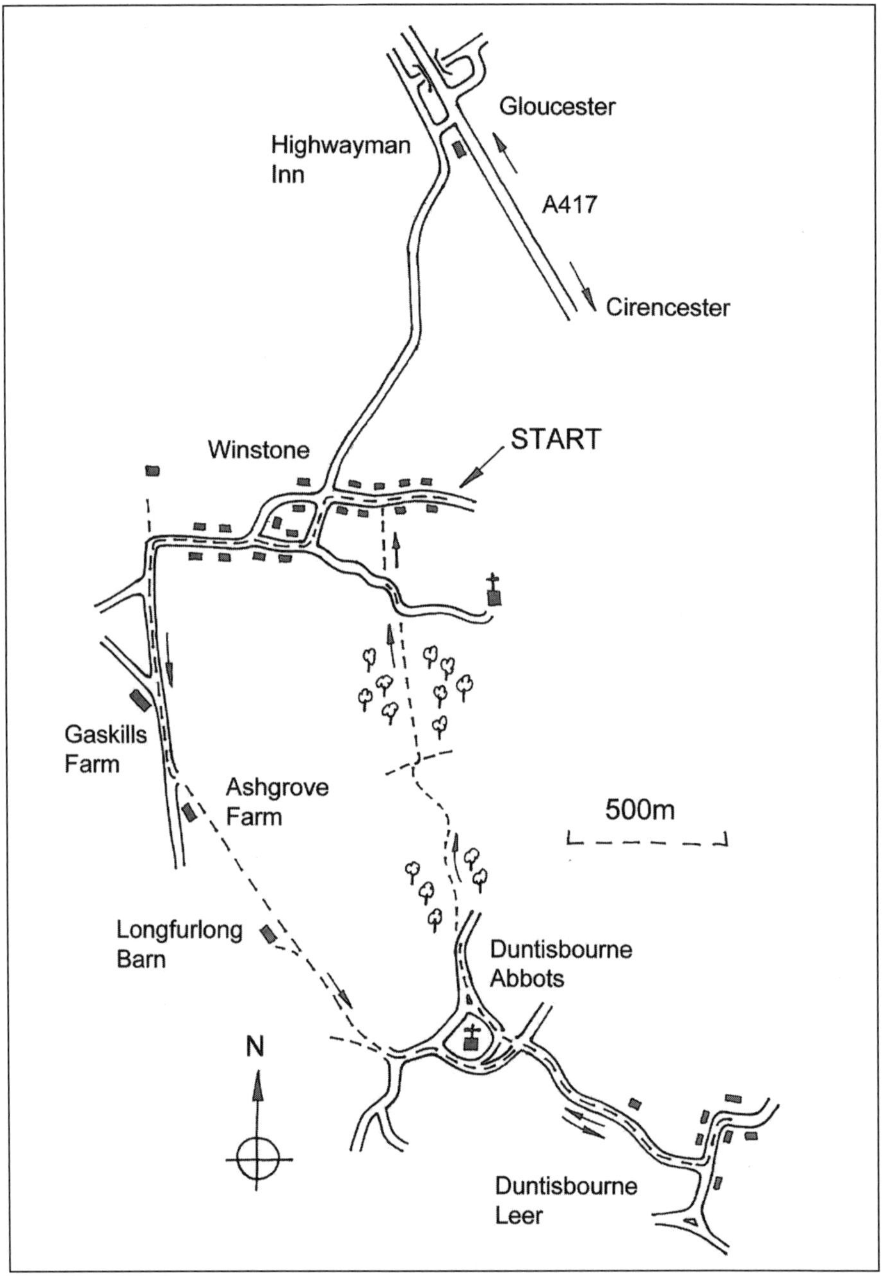
Gloucester
Highwayman Inn
A417
Cirencester
START
Winstone
Gaskills Farm
Ashgrove Farm
500m
Longfurlong Barn
Duntisbourne Abbots
N
Duntisbourne Leer

leaves are better able to survive the winter. Fir, pine and spruce are all evergreen conifers - look out for cones along the path. Look at how dry the ground is underneath the trees. Trees drink a lot of water through their roots. For instance, a Birch tree can absorb 30 gallons of water every day - that's almost two bath-fulls!

Eventually you arrive at a road junction on the outskirts of Duntisbourne Abbots, where you turn left signposted Birdlip and Cirencester. After 200m take a right fork, and follow the road down past the churchyard. As you pass Sundial Cottage, look back at the sundial on its gable end.

✓Long ago, clocks were very expensive, and people used a sundial instead. As the sun moves across the sky, the shadow cast by the arm moves across the face of the wall allowing you to tell the time. There would have been some numbers painted onto the wall but these have gone now. The sun rises in the morning and falls in the afternoon, but at midday the sun is directly overhead and your shadow is very short.

Q3 Does your shadow get longer in the morning or shorter?

Turn right at the bottom of the hill onto a road that is marked 'unsuitable for motors'. Pause by the telephone box and look at the old chapel on the left with its black and white paintwork.

Q4 There is another weather vane on the chapel. What can you see on this one?
Q5 This road is unsuitable for what?

✓A ford is a place where a stream is so shallow it can be crossed without needing a bridge.

Continue along the lane to the ford.

✓Many years ago when people travelled around on a horse and cart a lane like this was useful for washing the cartwheels and the horses' hooves.

Soon the stream disappears near a house.

Q6 What is the house called? (Clue: look at the gate.)

The ford at Duntisbourne Leer

Continue up the hill to Duntisbourne Leer and turn left at the T-junction. Follow the road down the hill and round a sharp bend.

This is as far as we go but if you have your camera, cross the ford and look back for a classic Cotswold view. The pretty stream almost laps at the doors of the nearby cottages creating an idyllic scene. Head back the way you came but before you leave this delightful spot, look up at the gable end of the house facing you. This used to be a barn with a dovecote above it, but now the birds have gone it has become a cottage.

✓The pattern of holes in the wall near the roof is called a dovecote. They were built as a place for pigeons and doves to make their nests because many years ago people would eat the birds and their eggs. There was so much birds mess at the bottom of the wall that it was used a bit like horse manure to help things grow in the garden. The birds could be a pest when the farmers were sowing their crops in the field because they would eat the seed.

Q7 How many holes can you see?

Return the way you came and walk back up the hill turning right where signposted 'unsuitable for motors'. Re-trace your steps past the ford to reach

Duntisbourne Abbots and the telephone box you saw earlier. To the left of the telephone box, behind a fence, is the village spring.

✓ If you lived here in Victorian times, one of your first jobs in the morning would have been to come down here to fetch a bucket of water for washing and drinking. It was a good place to meet your friends who were all doing the same thing. About 70 years ago, the cottages were all connected to mains water which meant you just had to turn on a tap like you do now. This was much easier but people missed the chance to gossip round the village spring.

Look at the sign attached to the fence.

Q8 What year was the gate opened?

From here, don't turn left or right, but cross the road to find a metalled path which narrows as it climbs past Davenport House. At the top of the grassy triangle, turn right onto a road which passes the churchyard.

Q9 Look at the weathervane on top of the church. Can you see what sits on top of it?

At the next junction bear right signposted Cirencester and Birdlip. Follow the road down the hill under the shade of some towering **beech** trees until, after about 150m, you find a farm gate on the left. Pass through this and follow a grassy path along a dry valley bottom. Look out for a water trough on the right.

✓ Cows use this water trough to drink from. It may be a bit muddy here because they are messy drinkers! They can drink as much as a bath full of water every day. See if you can see their footprints near the trough. They have big footprints with two 'toes'.

Q10 What is a baby cow called?

✓ You may see some piles of soil on the ground. These are molehills and are made by moles as they tunnel under the ground. Moles are about the size of a large mouse except they have big paws which they use as shovels for digging their holes. They live underground and can hardly see. They mainly eat worms and insects. Would you like to be a mole?

Eventually you reach the end of this dry valley where you look to the right for a stile next to a gate. After passing through the gate, turn sharp left to reach a track. Cross the track and make for a gate in the middle of a row of farm gates. Beyond this, the narrow path soon arrives at a field, where you follow its left hand boundary to reach another gate.

✓In summer look out for the meadow cranesbill, which grows about half a metre tall. They are easy to spot because their blue/violet flowers have five petals.

Also see if you can spot some bright red flowers with black centres growing in the crop or at the edge of the field. These are poppies. They only live for a summer, and in the autumn their seeds fall to the ground and wait for a chance to grow. Poppy seeds need light in order to start growing, but most get buried under leaves or soil. They sometimes have to wait for years before some disturbance brings them up into the sunlight. Here the farmer has ploughed the field and brought some poppy seeds to the surface. Some of these poppies have been waiting to grow since before you were born!

Beyond this, resume your journey along the narrow valley, which bends right before passing through an avenue of conifers. As you leave these behind, look for a magnificent spreading **sycamore** tree straight ahead on the far side of the field. Head for a stone stile to the left of this tree and after crossing it, turn left onto a road. Follow the road for a short distance as it passes a dovecote and a barn.

✓Although the dovecote holes have been filled in you can still see where they were.

Q11 How many holes were there in the dovecote?

✓It's not far now!

As the road bends left, take a footpath that leaves the road on the right, and follow the gritted path back up to Notch Road. At the top, turn right and walk back to the car.

Duntisbourne Checklist

- ☐ Horse shoe
- ☐ Horse
- ☐ Stone ball
- ☐ Stone mushroom
- ☐ Round window
- ☐ Tennis court
- ☐ Water trough
- ☐ A flooded road
- ☐ Duck
- ☐ Hen
- ☐ Wheeley bin

Walk 20. Guiting Power

Pretty woodland streams, stone foot-bridges and a quintessential Cotswold village to keep the grown-ups happy! No fewer than three fords on this walk which mean plenty of opportunities for a paddle -come prepared!

Distance	8km (5 miles)
Starting point	Guiting Power is 7 miles west of Stow on the Wold. From Kineton, turn onto a minor road sign-posted 'Roel Gate 3 ½ miles'. When you reach an un-fenced section of road, look for a walled car park on the left where an estate track crosses the road. Grid Reference: 084258 Postcode: GL54 5UZ
Short cut	Two, see text and dotted line on map
Terrain	A hilly walk over tracks, fields and footpaths which can be muddy after rain
Public toilets	None apart from those available to patrons of the pubs listed below
Refreshments	The Half-Way-House at Kineton. The Farmer's Arms and the Post Office at Guiting Power
Pushchairs	Not suitable
Leaf collection	Oak, beech, field maple, ash, sycamore, lime and Norway maple
Map	OS Explorer Map OL45

Guiting Power

Guiting Power is one of the prettiest and least altered villages in the Cotswolds. This is partly due to the Guiting Manor Amenity Trust, founded by wealthy benefactor Raymond Cochrane in the early 1970s. At this time the manor and village were in a state of disrepair but Cochrane rebuilt the cottages and fixed rents at peppercorn levels in an attempt to preserve a way of life that was fast disappearing. There is a memorial to him by the village green.

Guiting Manor was once a substantial farm called Woodhouse, so named because it backed onto Guiting Wood. It acquired the grander title when its fashionable Georgian frontage was added. This was retained when Cochrane completely re-built the house. He was something of a visionary, and it was his wish that after his death the house could become a foundation promoting wildlife conservation. The house is wonderfully situated: the combine harvesters can be seen working the distant hills in autumn, and in spring the lambs can be seen playing tag on the nearby parkland.

There is an interesting insight to the workings of medieval England in the church, where a plaque records the gift of bread from Woodhouse to the poor of the village.

The Walk

Cross the road and look for an estate track which is 'unsuitable for motors'. High up on the left is Guiting Manor. Follow the track as it passes to the right of an estate cottage.

Q1 What is the name of the cottage?

✓Most of the trees in this wood are oak. They lose their leaves every autumn and the wind blows them into large piles. Hedgehogs like to curl up among the warm dry leaves so if you are having a bonfire on November 5th, check that no hedgehogs have crawled under the sticks before you light it. Many hedgehogs die this way.

Have you noticed that in the spring there are fewer leaves on the ground? What happens to them all? They rot and break down, turning into soil which feeds other plants and trees. In nature, nothing is wasted.

In spring, you may hear something tapping on wood. This will be a woodpecker. It uses it's beak to make a hole in a tree trunk to nest in. You might also hear the clucking call of a pheasant which makes its nest on the ground. Pheasants are not good fliers and they spend most of their time walking around the wood looking for food. If they are frightened they will take off with a 'whirring' sound from their wings.

After about 1km you reach an old road where you turn right. After crossing the stream, follow the road up round a tight left hand bend. After climbing out of the valley, the old road bends left. Go straight on here along a track.

✓*Look out for some farm gates along the track. They have a postcode on them. You would need a big letter box for these!*

Q2 What is the postcode on the gate?

After cresting the hill you pass to the right of some magnificent stands of **beech** tree.

✓Beech trees can be recognised by their oval leaves and smooth bark. Like the oaks, they lose their leaves in the autumn and are called broad-leaved trees because their leaves are broad and flat. The conifers shed their needle-like leaves all year round and new ones grow all the time so they are never bare.

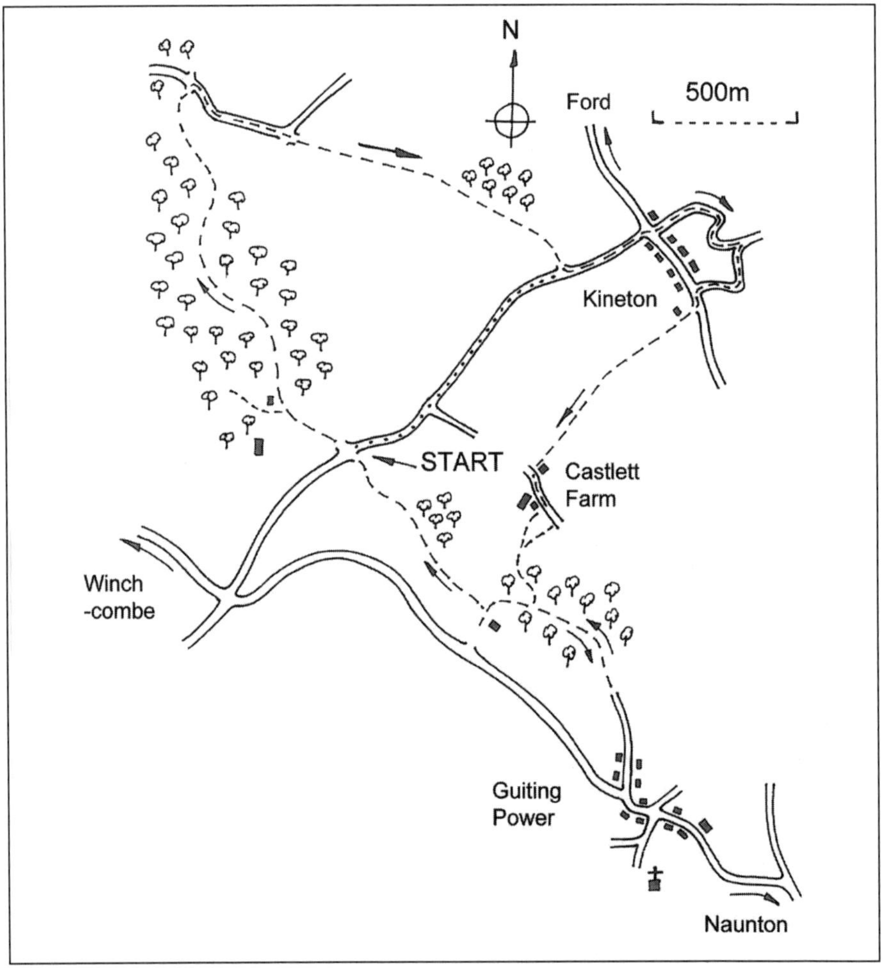

Beechnuts have prickly shells which split open to let the seeds out. Squirrels love them and in autumn they can be seen scampering through the branches to find them. If you look on the ground you will see many empty shells. Squirrels bury nuts so that they have some for later in the year. Sometimes they forget where they buried them (do you forget where you leave things?)

Look at the stone wall. This is called a 'dry stone wall' because there is no cement to glue the stones together. Each stone has to be carefully placed so it fits around the others. You can see it has fallen over in places. We will see a brand new dry-stone wall later on.

Q3 You are most likely to see a grey squirrel. What other squirrel lives in this country?

Eventually the track reaches a country lane where you turn left. Follow the road down to a T-junction where you turn right, immediately looking left for a lane that continues down into the valley of the Windrush.

Q4 This road is unsuitable for _____?

✓Look at the road sign. A ford is a place where a stream is so shallow it can be crossed without needing a bridge. Many towns grew up around fords and were named after them. Hereford is one, can you think of another?

At the bottom of the hill cross a stone bridge and turn right. This is a delightful spot for a paddle or a twig race in the clear cool water.

✓See if you can spot a mallard duck. The male is easy to see. He has a brown chest, a green head and a yellow bill. The female is light brown. They 'moult' in summer which means that some of their feathers fall out so they can keep cool in the warmer weather. Look out for their feathers in the grass. The feathers grow back as the weather gets colder.

Stay with the road as it bends left to climb away from the stream. Soon it reaches a road junction where you turn right to head back towards the village. Cross the next ford using a stone bridge which lies under the shade of a **field maple.**

Q5 How many arches does the bridge have?

Walk up the lane until it reaches a road junction. (*If you want to take the short cut, turn right here and walk to the Halfway House Inn. Beyond the inn, turn left onto a road signposted 'Roel Gate 3 ½ miles'. Stay with this road until you reach the start which lies beyond another ford!)*

Turn left at this road junction. Within a few metres look right for a path that leaves the road to pass to the left of a barn before reaching a field. Walk up the left hand side of the next two fields.

✓There is a small **ash** tree half way along the second field.

At the end of the second field, look for a gap in the hedgerow which allows you into the adjacent field and its stile. Beyond the stile, go straight on, passing to the right of a newly built dry stone wall.

✓The wall is a bit narrower at the top than at the bottom to stop it falling over. They last a very long time. Further along there is a water trough. Cows can drink up to a bath-full every day. Can you see a water pipe leading to the trough to keep it topped up? Imagine if you had to keep this full by carrying water to it in a bucket!

Continue along the path which is bounded by a fence until, as you near a green-roofed barn, you reach a stile in front of a hedgerow. Turn immediately

The ford at Kineton

left after the stile, and then right, passing between the hedge and a **sycamore** tree to enter the garden of a cottage. Just when you feel like an uninvited guest, a few steps take you down from the lawn onto a gravel drive. Follow this out of the garden to the road where you turn left.

Walk past Castlett Farm, and just as you leave the buildings behind, look to the right for a broad fenced path that heads down between the paddocks. The landowner wants the path moved further away from the farm, and has provided an alternative further up. This has caused some controversy locally but you needn't get involved, both routes take you to the other side of the farm. The path soon bends left near a **lime** tree before reaching a gate.

Beyond this, walk down through the trees to cross the bubbling Castlett brook to reach a junction of paths. (*A right turn will take you back to the start of the walk. Pick up the directions where shown **.*). Turn left here, and walk up a leafy path towards Guiting Power.

Soon the path gives way to tarmac, and eventually you reach a road junction. Cross the road and turn left, following the road round to the village green and its former post office, now a coffee shop.

Wander over to the far side of the village green and pause near the water pump.

Q6 The water comes out of the mouth of a _____.
Q7 There used to be a shop nearby. Can you see what it was called?
Q8 Down the road you can see the village pub. What is it called?

The nearby lane (sign-posted village hall and school) takes you to the parish church. This was substantially rebuilt in the 19th century but still retains its fine Norman arch around the south doorway.

Return the way you came, leaving the village behind and taking the path down through the trees to the junction of paths you left earlier.

** Go straight on now, climbing up through the trees along a stony path that soon reaches some quarry buildings. Turn right by the power line and follow this broad sandy track back to the start.

✓Look at the crops in the nearby fields. These are now harvested by machine. Many years ago they would have been cut down and gathered in by hand. The whole family would be up as soon as it was light, and would work until the sun went down. If there was a full moon, the last of the crop would be gathered in by moonlight! Imagine being so tired that you fell asleep eating your supper and had to be carried to bed!

After about 500m you pass a copse populated mainly by **ash** and **Norway maple**.

✓Ash trees seeds hang in clusters during the winter and don't fall to the ground until spring. Its wood is strong and bendy and is used to make oars, hockey sticks and handles for tools.

We are nearly back to the car!

Guiting Power Checklist

☐ Nesting box	☐ Stone bridge
☐ Fallen tree	☐ Horse
☐ Wooden bridge	☐ Stone ball
☐ Duck	☐ Red telephone box

Walk 21. Sapperton

A leafy walk along the tow-path of a disused canal, which follows the River Frome up to Sapperton and its tunnels. This walk has something for everyone: industrial archaeology, views, woodland streams, and charming Cotswold cottages.

Distance	8km (5 miles)
Starting point	Sapperton lies 6 miles west of Cirencester. Look for two minor roads that leave the north side of A419 Stroud to Cirencester road near Frampton Mansell. Take the easterly option (sign-posted 'Village Hall') which heads into the village from Oxstalls Farm. After about 600m look for the Village Hall on the right, and park next to it on the road-side verge. Grid Reference: 923024 Postcode: GL6 8JB
Short cut	Yes, see text and dotted line on map
Terrain	A mixture of country lanes, tracks, fields and footpaths which can be muddy at times. One short but steep climb. There is a railway line early in the walk which will have to be crossed with care
Public toilets	None apart from those available to patrons of the pubs listed below
Refreshments	The Crown at Frampton, the Daneway at Chalford and the Bell at Sapperton
Pushchairs	Not suitable
Leaf collection	Field maple, oak, lime and beech
Map	OS Explorer Map 168

Sapperton and its tunnels

There was only one obstacle facing the Thames & Severn Canal Company when they embarked on their ambitious plan to build a canal between the Severn and the Thames: the Cotswolds. They took an enormous risk, because

Sapperton Canal Tunnel

not only did they decide to build the world's longest tunnel at 3.5km, but it had to be perfectly level! Over this distance even a gradient of 1 in 11,000 would have resulted in a foot more water at one end than the other and a risk of boats getting jammed against the roof. It opened in 1789 after 5 years of construction, and was so straight you could see right through it. Trade flourished, and the canal remained in use until the early 1900s before being abandoned in 1927.

Another man who could plot a straight line was local astronomer Charles Mason, who resolved a border dispute between the Northern and Southern (Dixie) United States. He accurately surveyed the border line which now bears his name – The Mason Dixon Line.

Earlier in his career he had been assistant astronomer at Greenwich, and it was while working there that he tragically lost his first wife Rebekah. She is buried in Sapperton churchyard.

The Walk

Walk down into the village and bear right at the road junction to reach the church. Turn left here signposted Oakridge, and within 30m turn right onto a path that drops down past the churchyard.

Q1 What animal is standing on top of the church spire?

Soon you join a road which drops down to a junction where you turn right. Look immediately left for a path that descends steeply down to a railway line.

Q2 What must you beware of here?

This is a busy line so cross quickly but carefully. Continue downhill, and walk to the left of a cottage roof to reach an old canal basin.

✓The ditch in front of you was once a canal, a sort of man made river. Boats were towed along it by horses, which is why the path alongside the canal is called a towpath. A toll-keeper lived in the cottage nearby and it was his job to collect a toll, a charge for using the canal. Can you see that its windows are angled so the toll keeper can see both ways along the canal? This is to stop a boat sneaking past without paying!

Turn right and follow the towpath past the cottage taking care not to get too close to the lock on the left. Soon the track bears right, but you keep straight on, passing through a gate which allows you to stay with the towpath. Eventually you reach an old canal bridge. Pause by the arch on the far side.

✓Can you see a couple of grooves worn into the stone over many years by the rope used by the horse to tow the boat?

Soon afterwards you enter the Siccaridge Wood Nature Reserve, with its information board. In springtime the ground is carpeted with bluebells, wild garlic and wood anemones.

✓Wild garlic has long pointed leaves with little white flowers. Rub their leaves between your fingers to release a strong garlic smell. Near the water there are many reeds and waterside plants which provide food and shelter for insects like dragonflies and water boatmen. In March look around the stems of reeds for frog spawn, which is a sort of clear jelly containing the frogs' eggs. They hatch out into tadpoles which grow tails and later turn into frogs. In summer, you'll see the flowers of the yellow flag iris which love being near the water.

Eventually you reach a footbridge over an old lock which takes you to the other side of the canal. Five locks later the Daneway Inn is reached by carefully crossing a road.

✓This pub was originally a row of cottages built for the canal workers. When they left it became a pub called the Bricklayers' Arms.

Q3 What is the pub called now?

Walk through the pub car park and pick up the tow path at the far end. Soon the path reaches Sapperton Tunnel.

✓The canal workers built a tunnel to take the canal under the hill. The horse would be untied and taken over the top of the hill to the other end of the tunnel to wait for the boat to come through. The crew would get the boat through the tunnel by lying on the top of the boat, and pushing against the tunnel roof with their legs. It would take five hours to do this so there was often a long queue of boats here.

To a bat, an old canal tunnel is like an artificial cave. It's an ideal spot to hide during the day and hibernate in during the winter. They come out as it gets dark to feed on insects.

Q4 How many insects does our smallest bat, the Pipistrelle, eat each night? 300? 1,000? 3,000?

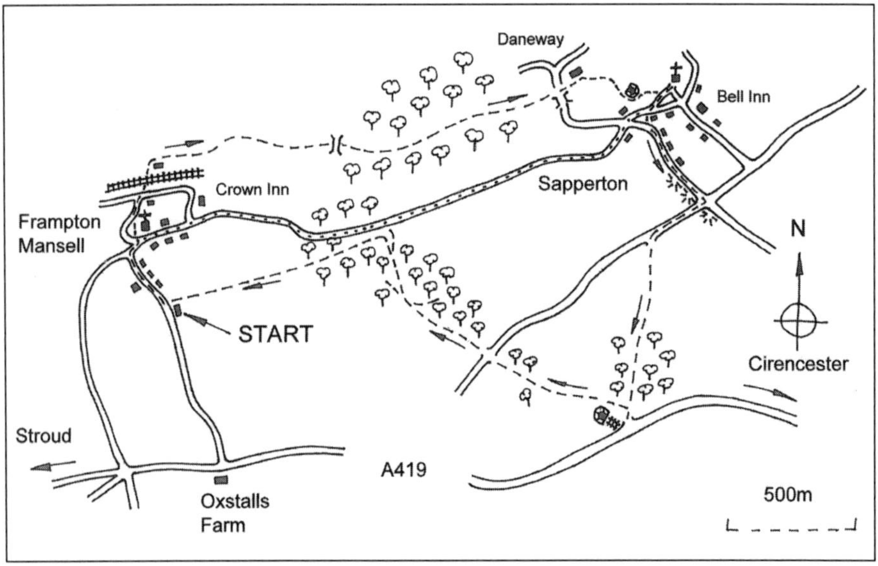

Walk up around the tunnel portal to find a stile under the shade of a **field maple**. Beyond this, look slightly right, and climb up past a gnarled **oak** tree to reach a gate beyond a water trough at the top of the field. Walk up into the village of Sapperton, and turn left at the road which takes you to the parish church of St Kenelm. Turn left here onto a path, which soon arrives at the churchyard gate. Walk past the church porch to reach a 'table top' tomb. Beyond this are two flat tombstones, the second one with the metal plaque is the grave of Rebekah Mason (see introduction to walk).

Sacred to the Remains of Rehekah,
Wife of Charles Mason, Junr., A.R.S.
With the greatest serenity of mind
She departed this Life the 13th of February1759,
at Greenwich, in Kent, in the 31st Year of her age.

Q5 Up to the right of the church door is the head of which animal?

✓The trees near the path are yews. They live for a very long time, sometimes more than 1,000 years. Its wood has been used to make things like spears, bows (and arrows), combs pegs and bowls. The yew tree is an evergreen which means it keeps it leaves all year round.

Q6 How many yews can you see in the church yard?

Walk through the yews and out of the church yard. The Bell Inn can be reached by going straight on, but if you want to continue with the walk turn right, and follow the road through the village. Soon you arrive at the village school where you turn left onto a path near a bus stop. (*If you want to take the short cut, stay with the road to reach a cross-roads. Continue across it to find a road sign-posted Frampton Mansell. On reaching Frampton, turn left near the church to reach the start of the walk.*)

Walk up the path and stop near Barn Cottage.

Q7 There's a little metal face on the wall, what is it?

Before municipal fire brigades were formed, they were operated by the Insurance Companies. This house was originally insured by the Sun Company, who placed this Fire Mark on the outside of the insured property to guide their fire brigade. The Sun Company was established in 1710 and still exists today as Royal & Sun Alliance. It's the oldest insurance company still bearing its original name.

Turn left at the main road and follow it past some **lime** trees until you reach the last house on the left near some speed limit signs. Pause here and look at the clump of **beech** trees on the right hand side of the road. Looking down the road you'll see another group about 150m away, and yet another just beyond the road junction. These mark the course of the canal.

✓When the workmen built the canal tunnel you saw earlier they dug holes from above the tunnel to help remove all the rubble. There was a hole under this group of trees. The rubble was piled up around the hole which became a bit of a mess, so the workers planted these beech trees on top of the rubble to make it look better. This tells us the canal tunnel is right beneath your feet (don't jump about!). See if you can impress the adults by telling them how old these trees are!

Q8 How old are these trees? (Clue: the canal was built in 1789.)

Continue to the road junction where you turn right signposted Cherington. After about 150m, turn left onto an old track which eventually passes through some woodland to reach a road. About 50m before the road however, turn right into the trees and pass some logs to reach the edge of the copse. Bear left to reach a wooden fence beyond which is a cutting and the portal of Sapperton railway tunnel. This was completed in 1845 and the railway soon began to take traffic away from the canal.

Q9 Can you see what colour bricks have been used to build the tunnel? (Don't go beyond the fence.)

✓These bricks are much harder, and last much longer than red bricks. Rainwater can get inside a red brick, making it crack when the frosts arrive in winter.

Before you leave, look at all the beech nut shells on the ground.

✓These would have contained nuts, but they have been eaten by squirrels. When there are too many to eat they will bury them for later in the year. Sometimes they forget where they buried them and the nuts remain in the soil to grow into new trees in the spring.

Q10 You are most likely to see a Grey Squirrel. What other squirrel lives in this country?

Return to the fence and, using it as a guide, head off across the field looking for a gap in the tree line on the far side. Here you pick up a grassy path which soon enters some woodland before reaching a brick-built ventilation chimney.

✓When the workmen built the railway tunnel they also dug down from above to help remove the rubble. This chimney was built around the hole. The trains that first used the tunnel made a lot of smoke so this chimney helped the smoke escape, otherwise the passengers would suffocate in the tunnel. Once more the tunnel is right beneath your feet so walk on tiptoes!

Continue to a road which is crossed carefully to pick up the path on the other side. Bear right at a fork to reach another ventilation shaft which seems to have been repaired using whatever was lying about.

Shortly after passing under a power line you take a left fork near a wall, ignoring the path ahead which drops down to a road. After occupying a leafy ledge above the road the path reaches a field. Go straight across this, passing through a gap in a boundary wall to reach Frampton and the start of the walk.

Sapperton Checklist

☐ Red telephone box	☐ Garden shed
☐ Fallen tree	☐ Tunnel
☐ Duck	☐ Bird table
☐ Hen	☐ Mirror
☐ Train	☐ A swing

Answers

Walk 1 Blockley
1. 1861
2. 1851
3. Wild Children
4. At all times
5. Six
6. Four
7. Man
8. J.R. Cayzer
9. 1953

Walk 2 Winchcombe
1. Seven
2. Two
3. 1984
4. 1887
5. Catherine Middleton, Duchess of Cambridge
6. 1891
7. Cockerel
8. Elizabeth
9. Rabbit
10. 1897

Walk 3 The Slaughters
1. Six - count the legs!
2. A Cockerel
3. Lion
4. 1875
5. £2
6. Elizabeth
8. 88
9. 1846

Walk 4 Chalford
1. 1742
2. 1952
3. Red
4. 17 tons
5. ... Trains
6. ... Western Railway
7. Four
8. Cockerel

Walk 5 Cirencester
1. 1802
2. Two
3. Elizabeth
4. Cygnet
5. Cockerel
6. ... tongue!
7. Cirencester
8. Two, and two more round the corner

Walk 6 Chipping Campden
1. Twelve
2. Eight
3. 1832
4. 1871
5. 1897
6. Elizabeth
7. Two birds
8. 1977

Walk 7 Stow on the Wold
1. 1883
2. 1917
3. Cockerel
4. Cygnet
5. Owl
6. 1937
7. 2004
8. 947
9. Cockerel

Walk 8 Tetbury
1. Two Lions
2. Acorn
3. Three
4. 1836
5. Fish (dolphins)
6. Camilla
7. Three feet
8. Cockerel
9. 1884
10. Sleep

Walk 9 Fairford

1. 17 years old, quite old for a cat.
2. 2008
3. 1972
4. The Queen's Head
5. No. Flies only bite, they can't sting.
6. Caterpillar
7. Bobby
8. Walnut tree
9. 1887
10. River Coln
11. 1827

Walk 10 Bourton on the Water

1. 1902
2. Two
3. Cygnet
4. Duke of Wellington
5. Fox
6. Foal
7. Three
8. Water
9. Gosling
10. 1955
11. 1888

Walk 11 Adlestrop

1. 1849
2. A red squirrel
3. Queen Elizabeth
4. 47 years
5. One minute
6. Thirty gallons!
7. Acorn
8. Ten mph
9. Fourteen
10. Lavender
11. Eight tons
12. 1728
13. The Fox

Walk 12 Bibury

1. Cygnet
2. Swan
3. Twelve
4. Lamb
5. Hazelnut
6. Acorn
7. Foal

Walk 13 Naunton

1. 1748
2. Lewis Carroll
3. 1850
4. Cockerel
5. 1840
6. Oxford
7. 100,000
8. Acorn
9. Longer

Walk 14 Miserden

1. 1914
2. 1866
3. 100,000!
4. No. Flies only bite, they can't sting.
5. ... Gate
6. Acorn
7. Red
8. 1867
9. Longer

Walk 15 Painswick

1. Pedestrians
2. About 1820 when the road was constructed
3. Foal
4. Cynet
5. Elizabeth
6. Acorn
7. Nineteen
8. 1840
9. Heart
10. Seven

Walk 16 Daglingworth

1. Acorn
2. A pound coin!
3. Dog
4. Six
5. 1756
6. Six million
7. Three feet
8. Longer
9. Red

Walk 17 Uley

1. A bird
2. A ship
3. Regent
4. 1981
5. The Old Crown
6. Queen Elizabeth
7. A pig, the emblem of Uley Brewey
8. 1833
9. The Kings Head

Walk 18 Northleach

1. 1836
2. Spots
3. Cockerel
4. A crown
5. A calf
6. Two
7. Elizabeth
8. A tractor
9. Combine

Walk 19 Duntisbourne

1. 10am
2. A man riding a horse
3. Shorter
4. A horse
5. Motors
6. Longford
7. 46
8. 1985
9. Cockerel
10. Calf
11. 16

Walk 20 Guiting Power

1. Pump Bottom Cottage
2. GL54 5UP
3. Red squirrel
4. Motors
5. Three
6. Lion
7. Watsons
8. The Farmers Arms

Walk 21 Sapperton

1. Cockerel
2. Trains
3. The Daneway
4. 3,000!
5. Lion
6. Nine
7. The Sun
8. Any answer over 200 would be ok!
9. Technically they're blue, but they now look grey
10. Red

Also from Sigma Leisure:

Discover The Cotswolds town and country walks

Roy Woodcock

The 20 walks included in this book are chosen to see a wide range of Cotswold towns and villages and to walk across stunning scenery and visit many historic locations.These walks are not intended to be strenuous. Although a steep hill may be encountered in a few of the walks, for example Wotton-under-Edge, they are mostly gentle walks, and quite short in mileage. The aim is to provide an interesting day out with a short walk, a good lunch in one of the many pubs, and a visit to a feature of interest in the area.

£8.99

Walks in the Forest of Dean and Wye Valley

Dave Meredith

The Forest of Dean and Wye Valley is a paradise for both the keen rambler and the casual stroller. The 22 walks described in this book are along easy footpaths taking you to spectacular viewpoints, along woodland glades carpeted with bluebells, daffodils and foxgloves, and under the dappled shade of its golden autumn canopy.

£8.99